BARTON'S

COMIC RECITATIONS

BARTON'S

COMIC RECITATIONS

AND

HUMOROUS DIALOGUES.

CONTAINING

A VARIETY OF COMIC RECITATIONS IN PROSE AND POETRY
AMUSING DIALOGUES, BURLESQUE SCENES, ECCEN-
TRIC ORATIONS AND STUMP SPEECHES,
HUMOROUS INTERLUDES, AND
LAUGHABLE FARCES.

DESIGNED FOR

SCHOOL COMMENCEMENTS AND AMATEUR THEATRICALS,

EDITED BY

JEROME BARTON.

Granger Index Reprint Series

BOOKS FOR LIBRARIES PRESS
FREEPORT, NEW YORK

First Published 1871
Reprinted 1971

INTERNATIONAL STANDARD BOOK NUMBER:
0-8369-6279-6

LIBRARY OF CONGRESS CATALOG CARD NUMBER:
79-167474

PRINTED IN THE UNITED STATES OF AMERICA

CONTENTS.

	PAGE
INTRODUCTION	5
PROLOGUE	7
THE STAGE-STRUCK HERO	9
HERE SHE GOES—AND THERE SHE GOES	11
PASTOR M'KNOCK'S ADDRESS	15
OLD SUGAR'S COURTSHIP	18
THE BACHELOR'S REASONS FOR TAKING A WIFE	21
THE SPANISH VALET AND THE WAITING MAID	22
THE JACKDAW OF RHEIMS	25
JONATHAN AND THE ENGLISHMEN	29
ARTEMUS WARD'S TRIP TO RICHMOND	30
THE AUCTIONEER AND THE LAWYER	32
MR. AND MRS. SKINNER	34
THE BACHELOR AND THE BRIDE	39
THE DRUNKARD AND HIS WIFE	42
A WESTERN LAWYER'S PLEA AGAINST THE FACT	43
READING A TRAGEDY	44
CAST-OFF GARMENTS	45
HOW TO CURE A COUGH	48
THE SOLDIER'S RETURN	49
THE COUNTRYMEN AND THE ASS	51
COME AND GO	53
HOW THEY POP THE QUESTION	54
THE CLEVER IDIOT	56
THE KNIGHTS; OR, BOTH RIGHT AND BOTH WRONG	57
HOW THE LAWYER GOT A PATRON SAINT	60
JOSH BILLINGS ON LAUGHING	61
THE NIGHT AFTER CHRISTMAS	62
A CHANGE OF SYSTEM	64
THE CITIZEN AND THE THIEVES	90
BOGGS'S DOGS	91

CONTENTS.

PAGE

THE SMACK IN SCHOOL.................................. 92

THE TINKER AND THE MILLER'S DAUGHTER.................. 93

AN ORIGINAL PARODY................................... 95

THE PARSONS AND THE CORKSCREW........................ 96

THE OLD GENTLEMAN WHO MARRIED A YOUNG WIFE........... 97

THE STAGE-STRUCK DARKEY..............................101

GOODY GRIM *versus* LAPSTONE.........................104

THE WOMAN OF MIND...................................109

NURSERY REMINISCENCES...............................111

A MARTYR TO SCIENCE.................................113

LODGINGS FOR SINGLE GENTLEMEN.......................132

THE FARMER AND THE COUNSELLOR.......................134

THE PUGILISTS.......................................135

HOW PAT SAVED HIS BACON.............................138

THE IRISH DRUMMER...................................140

MIKE HOOTER'S BEAR STORY............................141

THE CRITIC..145

MR. CAUDLE WANTS A " LATCH-KEY".....................147

KUMBUGGING A TOURIST................................150

THE WIDOW'S VICTIM..................................164

JOSH BILLINGS ON THE MULE...........................170

THE TINKER AND THE GLAZIER..........................171

WONDERFUL DREAM.....................................174

A NEW OCCASIONAL ADDRESS............................175

AN OCCASIONAL PROLOGUE..............................176

ADDRESS ON CLOSING A PERFORMANCE....................177

A PROLOGUE..177

EPILOGUE..179

FINALE..180

INTRODUCTION.

WEEPING Philosophers there were of old,
Down whose long faces tears incessant rolled,
Fellows whose eyes, like mountain torrents' beds,
Ran o'er with freshets from their *fountain heads*—
Water deciding then—as now we see,
Each body's true *specific gravity*.
If of that whimpering sect one wretch remain
This book will cure his " water on the brain,"
Or change its source, and irrigate his eyes
With gushes born of laughter, not of sighs.
The widow Niobe, of bygone years,
Whom the gods *literally* " dissolved in tears,"
Reading this volume would her woes have spurned
Or, her grief lightened, to a rainbow turned!

Culled from all sources, here the flowers of wit,
Into a garland for the gay are knit,
And blossoms Humor in his chaplet weaves,
Lend an enrapturing richness to the leaves.
Not ancient quirks from Joseph Miller's mill,
But bran-new jests, the sparkling pages fill;
Puns that would make an undertaker smile,
Or cheer a miser who had lost his pile;
Stories so full of fun, the veriest bore
Must catch their point, and, tickled by it, roar;

Dramatic scenes, that in the evening read,
Will send the hearer side-shaken to bed;
Speeches, reported by the Comic Muse,
That fire all Laughter's batteries like a fuse,
And rhythmic hits, so whimsical and terse
That Satire's self seems grinning from each verse.

"Business is business;" but its toil and care,
By Mirth unlightened, who on earth could bear?
The day-fight o'er, its turmoil and its fret,
The mind, unharrassed, hastens to forget,
And the heart—torpid 'mid the jostling throng—
Bounds to the touch of Humor, Wit and Song.
Then turn the gas on, close the shutters tight,
Part the blank darkness from the inner light,
And cabined snugly in the Social Ark,
Set sail with Momus for your Patriarch.
This book's his chart, and stand by it and him
On seas of merriment prepare to swim,
With sheets outspread, a joyous household band,
Bound, with ligh hearts, to Laughter's happy land.

But, "hold, enough!" the nervous reader cries,
This preface long detains me from the prize.
Good wines no "bush" to advertise them need,
And wit, if genuine, for itself can plead.
Right, reader, right! Adieu, proceed alone,
The book's before you—exit *chaperone*.

                                        J. B.

PROLOGUE

———————

THE Court's assembled—no grave court of law
With critic ears for every verbal flaw,
But a gay group whose members every one
Have vowed allegiance to immortal Fun,
Nor mean—we see it in your eyes—to blame
The Junior Counsel speaking in his name.

We shall not cite a Marshall or a Kent
For musty rule or solemn precedent ;
Our pleasant pleas on merrier grounds we base,
For on your risibles we rest our case.
Mirth is our client, and our action lies
Against the demons of the realm of sighs.
These we would nonsuit, and to gain our cause
We only ask, for verdict, your applause !
Smile on our efforts then, our zeal 'twill fan,
And throw a laugh in, sometimes, if you can.
We're up for trial—may the Comic elves
Help us work credit to *acquit ourselves.*

Wit's *vadi mecum* unto court we've brought,
Brimful of antidotes to tristful thought,
And as these recipes for gloom we quote—
Odd as the tints in Joseph's motley coat—

7

If we should fail to read with accent **true**,
Laugh at the text, and give to *that* it's due.

The court being ready—may it please the court
To hear the plaintiffs make their light report.
Our book's so full of quips in prose and rhyme,
Drawn from a source " one step from the sublime,"
We scarcely know what readings to select,
For gems while choosing, gems we must reject.
Would that our lips were like the fairy girl's
That dropt, when opened, solitaires and pearls—
Then should Wit's jewels, polished, rich and clear,
Dropped from our mouths, find grace in every ear.

No more o' that—here let excuses rest ;
To wing the hours with joy we'll do our best.
Friends are our audience—not sardonic pokes
Who make a practice of dissecting jokes,
And " accent," " gesture," " attitude," discuss,
Of honor *minus*, but of humbug *plus*.
Good-natured faces on all sides we see,
Ready to titter at each *jeu d'esprit*,
And knowing these to genial hearts akin
We'll close our prologue, and at once begin.

BARTON'S

COMIC RECITATIONS

AND

HUMOROUS DIALOGUES.

THE STAGE-STRUCK HERO.

ANONYMOUS.

A STAGE-STRUCK hero while at home,
  His Zanga oft would roar;
One day the servant-maid did come
  And gently ope'd the door.

"Woman, away!" aloud he cries,
  "I wish to be alone."
"I beg your pardon," she replies,
  "There's one below unknown."

He seized her hand, and that with speed,
  "Oh, Isabella, dear!
In tears! thou fool!" "Not I indeed!
  I seldom shed a tear."

"But what's the meaning of all this!"
  "I'll tell thee." "Well, sir, well!"
"But! be thou plunged in hell's abyss
  "If it thou e'er shouldst tell!"

" You terrify me, sir.   Oh, Lord !
    What can the secret be !
I'll never tell—upon my word !
    No, never ! you shall see !

" What is it, sir ?   I long to know."
    " Know, then. I hate Alonzo ! "
" I understand—that man below ;
    How dare he trouble me so ? "

Away she went, and in good truth
    The man began to blame ;
In the meantime our spouting youth
    Richard the Third became.

" Here will I pitch my tent ! " he cries,
    And on the sofa stretch'd ;
The servant-maid again appear'd,
    For she his breakfast fetch'd.

" Give me a horse—bind up my wounds ! "
    He, jumping up, did call ;
The woman, startled at the sounds,
    Let all the tea-things fall !

In came the man. who having said,
    " Buckram, sir, I am ; "
" Off with his head ! " he cries aloud—
    " So much for Buckingham ! "

The man jump'd back, the woman scream'd,
    For both were sore afraid,
A bedlamite our spouter seem'd,
    And like Octavian said—

" I cannot sleep ! " " And wherefore pray ? "
    " The leaves are newly pull'd ! "
This said, the woman walk'd away
    Until his frenzy cool'd.

But Buckram gave his bill, and so
    He was resolved to stay ;

" I'll hug on't, will glut on't ! "—" Oh, no,
    I'd rather, sir, you'd pay ! "

" Reptile ! "—the exclamation shocks ;
    Great were the tailor's fears ;
" I'll dash thy body o'er the rocks ! "
    The man pulled out his shears.

" I'll grapple with thee thus," he cried—
    And soon the shears he won ;
The tailor was so terrified,
    That he thought fit to run.

HERE SHE GOES—AND THERE SHE GOES.

NACK.

Two Yankee wags, one summer day,
Stopped at a tavern on their way ;
Supped, frolicked, late retired to rest,
And woke to breakfast on the best.

The breakfast over, Tom and Will
Sent for the landlord and the bill ;
Will looked it over ; " Very right—
But hold ! what wonder meets my sight ?
Tom ! the surprise is quite a shock ! "
" What wonder ? where ? " " The clock ! the clock ! "

Tom and the landlord in amaze
Stared at the clock with stupid gaze,
And for a moment neither spoke ;
At last the landlord silence broke :

" You mean the clock that's ticking there ?
I see no wonder, I declare ;
Though may be, if the truth were told,
'Tis rather ugly—somewhat old ;
Yet time it keeps to half a minute,
But, if you please, what wonder's in it ? "

"Tom, don't you recollect," said Will,
"The clock in Jersey near the mill,
The very image of this present,
With which I won the wager pleasant?"
Will ended with a knowing wink—
Tom scratched his head, and tried to think.
"Sir, begging pardon for inquiring,"
The landlord said, with grin admiring,
"What wager was it?"

        "You remember,
It happened, Tom, in last December,
In sport I bet a Jersey Blue
That it was more than he could do,
To make his finger go and come
In keeping with the pendulum,
Repeating, till one hour should close,
Still ' *here she goes—and there she goes* '—
He lost the bet in half a minute."

"Well, if I would, the deuce is in it!"
Exclaimed the landlord; "try me yet,
And fifty dollars be the bet."
"Agreed, but we will play some trick
To make you of the bargain sick!"
"I'm up to that!"

        "Don't make us wait;
Begin, the clock is striking eight."
He seats himself, and left and right
His finger wags with all his might,
And hoarse his voice, and hoarser grows,
With " *here she goes—and there she goes!* "

"Hold!" said the Yankee, "plank the ready!"
The landlord wagged his fingers steady,
While his left hand, as well as able,
Conveyed a purse upon the table.
"Tom, with the money let's be off!"
This made the landlord only scoff;

He heard them running down the stair,
But was not tempted from his chair;
Thought he, " The fools ! I'll bite them yet !
So poor a trick shan't win the bet."
And loud and loud the chorus rose
Of *" here she goes—and there she goes !"*
While right and left his finger swung,
In keeping to his clock and tongue.

His mother happened in. to see
Her daughter ; " Where is Mrs. B——?
When will she come, as you suppose ?
Son !"
  " Here she goes—and there she goes !"
" Here ! where ? "—the lady in surprise
His finger followed with her eyes ;
" Son, why that steady gaze and sad ?
Those words—that motion—are you mad ?
But here's your wife—perhaps she knows,
And "—
  " Here she goes—and there she goes !"

His wife surveyed him with alarm,
And rushed to him and seized his arm ;
He shook her off, and to and fro
His fingers persevered to go,
While curled his very nose with ire,
That *she* against him should conspire,
And with more furious tone arose
The *" here she goes—and there she goes !"*

" Lawks ! " screamed the wife, " I'm in a whirl !
Run down and bring the little girl ;
She is his darling, and who knows
But "—
  " Here she goes—and there she goes !"

" Lawks ! he is mad ! What made him thus ?
Good Lord ! what will become of us ?
Run for a doctor—run—run—run—
For Doctor Brown, and Doctor Dun,

And Doctor Black, and Doctor White,
And Doctor Grey, with all your might."

The doctors came, and looked and wondered,
And shook their heads, and paused and pondered,
Till one proposed he should be bled,
" No—leached you mean," the other said—
" Clap on a blister," roared another,
" No—cup him "—" No—trepan him, brother ! "
A sixth would recommend a purge,
The next would an emetic urge,
The eighth, just come from a dissection,
His verdict gave for an injection ;
The last produced a box of pills,
A certain cure for earthly ills ;
" I had a patient yesternight,"
Quoth he, " and wretched was her plight,
And as the only means to save her,
Three dozen patent pills I gave her,
And by to-morrow, I suppose
That "—
          " *Here she goes—and there she goes !* "

" You all are fools," the lady said,
The way is, just to shave his head,
Run, bid the barber come anon "—
" Thanks, mother," thought her clever son,
" *You* help the knaves that would have bit me,
But all creation shan't outwit me ! "
Thus to himself, while to and fro
His finger perseveres to go,
And from his lips no accent flows
But " *here she goes—and there she goes !* "

The barber came—" Lord help him ! what
A queer customer I've got ;
But we must do our best to save him—
So hold him, gemmen, while I shave him ! "
But here the doctors interpose—
" A woman never "—
          " *There she goes !* "

But tak' ye special care o' thinking
That I wud hae ye always drinking !

" Then after dinner very soon,
And just to keep the victual doon,
And up the gay joy of the feast,
I'd hae ye tak' a gill at least ;
But mind and dunna noo be thinking
I recommend ye always drinking !
And i' the afternoon, d'ye see,
Mix still a wee drap wi' your tea ;
This practice is o' muckle service,
And certainly makes tea less nervous ;
But dinna ye, my friends, be thinking
By this I'd hae ye always drinking !
Pray ne'er neglect, whate'er be said,
A noggin 'fore ye gang to bed ;
Ye'll sleep the sounder a' the nicht,
And wake refresh'd at morning licht.
So this, my friends, I think we may
Indulge in safely ev'ry day ;
But dinna always be a thinking
That I wud hae ye always drinking !

" So but confine yoursels to this,
And naething will be much amiss ;
And recollect that men of sense
Still use the greatest temperance.
Bear this in mind, and ye'll stand fair to
Escape some ills that man is heir to,
And by this plan your doctor's bill
Will lighter be for draught and pill.
'Tis true expenses will increase,
For beef and mutton, ducks and geese,
But stomachs must hae mony faults
That like na sic food mair than salts.
Few men wud rather, that can chuse,
Their siller spend in drugs than shoes.
But every day, if you get foo,
Depend upon't, at last ye'll rue.

Woe to the man in youthful prime,
That wastes his siller thus, and time;
He'll sair repent and wail the day,
When time has turned his locks to gray.
So tak' na mair o' drink or food
Than what will do the body good:
Of my advice but mak' a proof,
And then ye'll dee quite weel enough."

OLD SUGAR'S COURTSHIP.

ROSS.

" THE ony objection ever made to me in this arr county, as a legislatur', was made by the wimmin' 'cause I war a *bachelor*, and I never told you afore why I *re*-mained in the state of number *one*—no fellar stays single *pre*-meditated, and, in course, a handsum fellar like me, who all the gals declar' to be as enticin' as a jay bird, warn't goin' to stay alone, ef he could help it.

" I did see a creatur' once, named *Sofy Mason*, up the Cum-berland, nigh unto Nashville, Tennes-*see*, that I took an or-ful hankerin' arter, and I sot in to lookin' anxious fur mat-rimony, and gin to go reglar to meetin', and took to dressin' tremengeous finified, jest to see ef I could get her good opinion. She did git to lookin' at me, and one day, comin' from meetin', she was takin' a look at me a kind of shy, just as a hoss does at something he's scared at, when arter champin' at a distance fur awhile, I sidled up to her, and blarted out a few words about the sarmin'—she said yes, but cuss me ef I knew whether that war the right answer or not, I'm a thinkin' she didn't know then, nuther ! Well, we larfed and talked a little all the way along to her daddy's, and thar I gin her the best bend I had in me, and raised my bran new hat as peert and *per*-lite as a minister, lookin' all the time so enticin' that I sot the gal tremblin'. Her old daddy had a powerful numerous lot of healthy niggers, and lived right adjinin' my place, while on to'ther side lived **Jake** Simons—a sneakin', cute varmint, who war wusser than **a** miser for stinginess; and no sooner did this cussed **sarpint** see me sidlin' up to Sofy, than he went to slikin' up too, **and** sot himself to work to cut me out. That arr wur a **struggle** ekill to the battle of Orleans. Furst sum new fixup of Jake's **w**ould take her eye, and then I'd sport suthin' that would outshine him, until Jake at last gin in tryin' to outdress me, and sot thinkin' of suthin' else. Our farms wur just the same number of acres, and we both owned three **niggers** apiece. Jake knew that Sofy and her dad kept a sharp **ey** out fur the main chance, so he thort he'd clar me out **by** buyin' another nigger; but I jest foller'd suit, and **bought** one the day arter he got his, so he had no advantage thar; he then got a *cow*, and so did I, and jest about then both **on** our *pusses* gin out. This put Jake to his wit's eend, and **I** war a wunderin' what in the yearth he would try next.

"We stood so, hip and thigh, fur about two weeks, both on us talkin' sweet to Sofy, whenever we could get her alone. I thort I seed that Jake, the sneakin' cuss, wur gittin' a mite ahead of me, 'cause his tongue wur so ily; howsever, I didn't let on, but kept a top eye on him. One Sunday mornin' I wur a leetle mite late to meetin', and when I got thar, the first thing I seed war Jake Simons, sittin' close bang up agin Sofy, in the same pew with her daddy!

"I biled a spell with wrath, and then tarned sour; I could taste myself! Thar they wur, singin' *himes* out of the same book. Je-e-eminy, fellers, I war so enormous mad that the new silk handkercher round my neck lost its color!

"Arter meetin', out they walked, linked arms, a smilin' and lookin' as pleased as a young couple at thar furst christenin', and Sofy tarned her cold shoulder at me so orful pinted, that I wilted down, and gin up right straight—Jake had her, thar wur no disputin' it! I headed toward home, with my hands as fur in my trousers pockets as I could push 'em, swarin' all the way that she war the last one would ever **git** a chance to rile up my feelin's. Passin' by Jake's **plantation,**

I looked over the fence, and thar stood an explanation of the matter, right facin' the road whar every one passin' could see it—his consarned *cow* was tied to a stake in the gardin' *with a most promisin' calf along side of her!* That *calf* jest soured my milk, and made Sofy think, that a feller who war allays gittin' ahead like Jake, wur a right smart chance for a lively husband! What is a cussed sight wusser than gittin' Sofy, war the fact, that he *borrowed that calf the night before from Dick Hardley!* Arter the varmint got Sofy hitched he told the joke all over the settle-*ment*, and the boys never seed me arterwards that they didn't ba-ah at me fur lettin' a *calf* cut me out of a gal's affections. I'd a shot Jake, but I thart it war a free country, and the gal had a right to her choice without bein' made a widder, so I jest sold out and travelled!"

THE BACHELOR'S REASONS FOR TAKING A WIFE.

ANONYMOUS.

GRAVE authors say and witty poets sing,
That honest wedlock is a glorious thing;
But depth of judgment most in him appears,
Who wisely weds in his maturer years.
Then let him choose a damsel young and fair,
To bless his age, and bring a worthy heir;
To sooth his cares, and free from noise and strife,
Conduct him gently to the verge of life;
Let sinful bachelors their woes deplore,
Full well they merit all they feel, and more;
Unawed by precepts, human and divine,
Like birds and beasts, promiscuously they join;
Nor know to make the present blessing last,
To hope the future, or esteem the past;
But vainly boast the joys they never tried,
And find divulged the secrets they would hide.
The married man may bear his yoke with ease,
Secure at once himself and heaven to please;

And pass his inoffensive hours away,
In bliss all night, and innocence all day.
Though fortune change, his constant spouse remains,
Augments his joys or mitigates his pains.
But what so pure, which envious tongues will spare ?
Some wicked wits have libelled all the fair.
With matchless impudence they style a wife
The dear-bought curse, and lawful plague of life ;
A bosom serpent, a domestic evil,
A night invasion, and a mid-day devil.
Let not the wise these slanderous words regard,
But curse the bones of every lying bard.
All other goods by Fortune's hand are given ;
A wife is the peculiar gift of heaven :
Vain Fortune's favors, never at a stay,
Like empty shadows glide and pass away ;
One solid comfort, our eternal w'fe,
Abundantly supplies us all our life.
This blessing lasts (if those who try say true)
As long as e'er a heart can wish—and longer too.
Our grandsire Adam, ere of Eve possessed,
Alone and even in Paradise unblessed,
With mournful looks the blissful scenes surveyed,
And wandered in the solitary shade :
The Maker saw, and pitying, did bestow
Woman, the last, the best of gifts below.
A wife ! ah, gentle deities, can he
That has a wife e'er feel adversity ?
Would men but follow what the sex advise,
All things would prosper, all the world grow wise!
'Twas by Rebecca's aid that Jacob won
His father's blessing from an elder son;
Abusive Nabal owed his forfeit life
To the wise conduct of a prudent wife
Heroic Judith, as old Hebrews show,
Preserved the Jews, and slew the Assyrian foe;
At Esther's suit the persecuting swo,d
Was sheathed, and Israel lived to bless the Lord.
Be charmed with virtuous joys, and sober life,
And try that Christian comfort called—a *wife !*

THE SPANISH VALET AND THE WAITING MAID.

A DUOLOGUE, FROM "THE WONDER."

Enter LISSARDO, L.

LISSAR. Was ever man so tormented? I saw that little gipsy, Flora, in close confab with Lazat, the miller's man—only once let me lay hold of him, I'll—by-the-by, this a very pretty ring my lady gave me—methinks a diamond is a vast addition to the finger of a gentleman. Egad, I have a pretty hand, it is very white and well-shaped—faith, I never noticed it so much before—it becomes a diamond ring as well as the first Don's in Andalusia.

FLORA. (*Without, calling.*) Lissardo! Lissardo!

LISSAR. Oh, the little minx—there she is calling for me; but I'll not answer.

Enter FLORA, R.

FLORA. Lissardo! Lissardo! I say—sure the fellow's dumb—ha! what do I see? a diamond ring—(*aside*) how the deuce did he get that? (*Aloud.*) You have got a very pretty ring there, Lissardo.

LISSAR. Um, the trifle's pretty enough; but the lady who gave it me is as beautiful as an angel, I assure you? (*Struts about and gives himself airs.*)

FLORA. (*Aside.*) I can't bear this—the lady! (*Aloud.*) What lady, pray?

LISSAR. There's a question to ask a gentleman.

FLORA. A gentleman indeed! why the fellow's spoil'd—is this your love for me, you brute?

LISSAR. Don't talk to me about love—didn't I catch you in close conversation with Lazat, the miller's man?

FLORA. There was no harm in that, I was only—

LISSAR. You were only—you're a base, ungrateful woman, and I've done with you—there, madam, you can take that tobacco stopper you gave me some time back, and stop your impertinent mouth with it.

FLORA. Indeed, sir! I believe I can keep tally with you in that respect; there, sir, there's the pretty little pincushion you gave me—take it. (*Throws it at him.*)

LISSAR. There's another little trifle—there, madam— (*gives a pocket-book*) it will serve you to write down an account of your false love. (*Throws it at her.*)

FLORA. Indeed, sir. (*Aside.*) The wretch so provokes me! (*Runs off, and returns with an apron full of letters.*) There, sir— there—you good-for-nothing brute—here's a bundle of your false scrawls for you, take them. (*Pelts him with the letters, he running away, and she after him.*)

LISSAR. I believe, madam, I can return the compliment. (*Taking out a packet and pelting her.*) And here's another precious article, take it. (*Lifts his stick and about to beat her.*)

FLORA. (*Throws herself into his arms.*) Beat me now, cruel Lissardo, do.

LISSAR. No, no!

Air.

LISSAR. Dear Flora, what would you be at?
　　　　　I don't wish to quarrel with you;
　　　　　You're in love with the miller, Lazat;
　　　　　If I meet him I'll cause him to rue.

The first time I set eyes on him, I'll give him a taste of as sharp a two-edged stiletto as any in all Madrid; and if he comes again to poach on my manor, I'll duck him in his own mill-pond, and he shall soon learn the difference between feeding on fish and feeding fish.

FLORA. If this is the way you try to make yourself agreeable, I shall, in future, take care to walk in some other path. (*Angrily.*) You are enough to provoke a saint—so you are! I've got anger enough from mother about you already; but never mind, it's the last time we shall ever meet —heigho! it's very provoking though—and I'm sure I didn't deserve this from you—oh! dear, oh! (*Crying.*)

LISSAR. I can't stand this—come, come, Flora dear.

FLORA.   You promise, but promise in vain,
               I love not to trifle like you;
               Your wish is to quarrel, that's plain,
               But I can be constant and true.

Well, good by, Lissardo—we part friends, I hope. (*Going.*)

LISSAR. Stop, stop, Flora! a word with you, before you go.

FLORA. It must be only one word then, for I have not time to hear another.

LISSAR. But suppose that one should prove agreeable—would you not then stop to hear another?

FLORA. Perhaps, in that case—(*hesitating.*) But what is the word?

LISSAR. A very short monosyllable, containing only four letters—this little word has been the cause of more quarrels, more misery, and more happiness, than all the words in the English language put together—what do you think of L, O, V, E?

FLORA. Oh! then I'm going in earnest.

LISSAR. (*Detaining her.*) What! without hearing the other three?

FLORA. Three words! what can they be?

LISSAR. A gold ring! (*Going.*) Now *I'm* in a hurry.

FLORA. (*Detaining him.*) Well, but, Lissardo, where can you be going? I can't think.

LISSAR. Only to your father—have I your leave?

FLORA. But are you really in earnest, indeed, and in truth? and will you tell him the *th. ee words?*

LISSAR. Certainly not—(FLORA *pouts*)—that is—without you desire it; and if you have no objections, I shall add a few more words about a church.

FLORA. Charming!

LISSAR. And a clerk to publish the banns of marriage.

FLORA. Delightful!

LISSAR. (*Archly.*) And we shall be as happy as the day is long—and then you know we shall have—

Air.

BOTH.   No more sighing, no more sorrow ;
       Let us happy pass the time ;
    To-day we'll sing, and dance to-morrow,
       And the bells shall merry chime.

                      (*Bells chime.*)

    Hark ! hark ! the bells so well keep time
    I love to hear their merry chime,
    The merry chime, the merry, merry chime.

THE JACKDAW OF RHEIMS.

BARHAM.

THE Jackdaw sat on the Cardinal's chair !
Bishop and abbot, and prior were there ;
    Many a monk, and many a friar,
    Many a knight, and many a squire,
With a great many more of lesser de_ree,—
In sooth a goodly company ;
And they served the Lord Primate on bended knee.
    Never, I ween,
    Was a prouder seen,
Read of in books, or dreamt of in dreams,
Than the Cardinal Lord Archbishop of Rheims !

    In and out
    Through the motley rout,
That little Jackdaw kept hopping about ;
    Here and there
    Like a dog in a fair,
    Over comfits and cates,
    And dishes and plates,
Cowl and cope, and rochet and pall,
Mitre and crosier ! he hopp'd upon all !
    With saucy air,
    He perch'd on the chair
Where, in state, the great Lord Cardinal sat
In the great Lord Cardinal's great red hat ;

And he peer'd in the face
Of his Lordship's Grace,
With a satisfied look, as if he would say,
" We two are the greatest folks here to-day ! "
And the priests, with awe,
As such freaks they saw,
Said, " The Devil must be in that little Jackdaw !'

The feast was over, the board was clear'd,
The flawl.s and the custards had all disappeared,
And six little singing-boys—dear little souls !
In nice clean faces, and nice white stoles,
Came, in order due,
Two by two,
Marching that grand refectory through !
A nice little boy held a golden ewer,
Emboss'd and fill'd with water, as pure
As any that flows between Rheims and Namur,
Which a nice little boy stood ready to catch
In a fine gol len hand-basin made to match.
Two nice little boys, rather more grown,
Carried lavender-water, and eau de Cologne ;
And a nice little boy, had a nice cake of soap,
Worthy of washing the hands of the Pope.
One little boy more
A napkin bore,
Of the best white diaper, fringed with pink,
And a Cardinal's hat mark'd in " permanent ink."

The great Lord Cardinal turns at the sight
Of these nice little boys dress'd all in white :
From his finger he draws
His costly turquois ' ;
And, not thinking at all about little Jackdaws,
Deposits it straight
By the side of his plate ;
While the nice little boys on his Eminence wait ;
Till, when nobody's dreaming of any such thing,
That little Jackdaw hops off with the ring !

> There's a cry and a shout,
> And a deuce of a rout,
And nobody seems to know what they're about,
But the monks have their pockets all turn'd inside out;
> The friars are kneeling,
> And hunting, and feeling
The carpet, the floor, and the walls, and the ceiling.
> The Cardinal drew
> Off each plum-colored shoe,
And left his red stockings exposed to the view
> He peeps, and he feels
> In the toes and the heels;
They turn up the dishes—they turn up the plates—
They take up the poker and poke out the grates—
> They turn up the rugs—
> They examine the mugs :—
> But, no !—no such thing ;
> They can't find THE RING!
And the abbot declared that, " when nobody twigg'd it,
Some rascal or other had popp'd in, and prigg'd it ! "

The Cardinal rose with a dignified look,
He call'd for his candle, his bell, and his book !
> In holy anger, and pious grief,
> He solemnly cursed that rascally thief!
> He cursed him at board, he cursed him in bed ;
> From the sole of his foot to the crown of his head ;
> He cursed him in sleeping, that every night
> He should dream of the devil, and wake in a fright;
> He cursed him in eating, he cursed him in drinking,
> He cursed him in coughing, in sneezing, in winking;
> He cursed him in sitting, in standing, in lying ;
> He cursed him in walking, in riding, in flying,
> He cursed him in living, he cursed him in dying !·
Never was heard such a terrible curse ! !
> But what gave rise
> To no little surprise,
Nobody seem'd one penny the worse.

The day was gone,
The night came on,
The monks and the friars they search'd till dawn,
When the sacristan saw,
On crumpled claw,
Come limping a poor little lame Jackdaw !
No longer gay,
As on yesterday ;
His feathers all seem'd to be turn'd the wrong way ;—
His pinions droop'd—he could hardly stand—
His head was as bald as the palm of your hand ;
His eye so dim,
So wasted each limb,
That, heedless of grammar, they all cried, "THAT'S HIM !—
That's the scamp that has done this scandalous thing !
That's the thief that has got my Lord Cardinal's ring !"
The poor little Jackdaw,
When the monks he saw,
Feebly gave vent to the ghost of a caw ;
And turn'd his bald head, as much as to say,
"Pray be so good as to walk this way !"
Slower and slower
He limp'd on before,
Till they came to the back of the belf.y door,
Where the first thing they saw,
'Midst the sticks and the straw,
Was the RING in the nest of that little Jackdaw !

Then the great Lord Cardinal call'd for his book,
And off that terrible curse he took ;
The mute expression
Served in lieu of confession,
And, being thus coupled with full restitution,
The Jackdaw got plenary absolution !
When those words were heard,
That poor little bird
Was so changed in a moment, 'twas really absurd,
He grew sleek and fat ;
In addition to that,

A fresh crop of feathers came thick as a mat !
      His tail waggled more
      Even than before ;
But no longer it wagg'd with an impudent air,
No longer he perch'd on the Cardinal's chair.
      He hopp'd now about
      With a gait devout ;
At matins, at vespers, he never was out;
And, so far from any more pilfering deeds,
He always seem'd telling the confessor's beads.
If any one lied—or if any one swore—
Or slumber'd in prayer-time and happen'd to snore,
      That good Jackdaw
      Would give a great " caw ! "
As much as to say, " Don't do so any more ! "
While many remark'd, as his manners they saw,
That they " never had known such a pious Jackdaw ! "
      He long lived the pride
      Of that country side,
And at last in the odor of sanctity died ;
      When, as words were too faint
      His merits to paint,
The conclave determined to make him a saint ;
And on newly-made saints and Popes, as you know,
It's the custom, at Rome, new names to bestow,
So they canonized him by the name of Jim Crow.

JONATHAN AND THE ENGLISHMEN.

ANONYMOUS.

On the plain of New Jersey, one hot summer's day,
  Two Englishmen, snug in a stage-coach, were vap'ring ;
A Yankee, who happen'd to travel that way.
  Took a seat alongside, and sat wond'ring and gaping.

Chockfull of importance (like every true Briton,
  Who knows British stars far outshine our poor Luna),
These cockneys found nothing their optics could hit on,
  But what was insipid or miserably puny.

Compared with the English, our horses were colts,
  Our oxen were goats, and a sheep but a lamb;
And the people! (poor blockheads) such pitiful dolts!
  Mere Hottentot children, contrasted with them!

Just then, a black cloud in the west was ascending;
  The lightning flash'd frequent, with horrible glare
When near and more near, a fierce tempest portending,
  The thunder rebellowed along the rent air.

An oak by the wayside Jove's bolt made a dash on,
  With a peal that knock'd horses and cockneys all flat;
" There, hang you! " cries Jonathan, quite in a passion,
  " Have you got better *thunder* in England than that? "

ARTEMUS WARD'S TRIP TO RICHMOND.

BROWNE.

It's putty plane to my mind that we earnt tu have Peas as long as the fite goes on. Not much. The sympathizin' Demos promist that these rebellion shood be over as soon as they was 'lected, an' they air doin' all in thar power to get it over—all over the North. You cood stick more loyalty in a chicken's ear than sich men possess.

The other day I 'pinted myself a committee ov the whole to go to Richmond an' see ef I coodent convins J. Davis ov the error of his ways, and persuade him to jine the Young Men's Christian Association. Sumthin' must soon be did to have the War stopt, or by the time it's ended the Northern Sympathizers will have no Southern Brethren, or no Constitootion, or no Declaration of Injypendence, or no nothing, or anything else. None. Whar cood we procoor G. Washingtons, J. Quincy Jeffersons, Thomas Adamses, and etsettery, to make another Constitootion and so 4th—the larst especially? Echo ansers—Whar? That's why the Blacks air taken sich good care ov that instroment—which reminds me ov a little incident, as A. L. obsarves.

But, I am goin' to tell you about me trip to the Capitol ov the Southern Conthieveracy. It was a bootiful mornin' that I started; nary a cloud obskewered the Orb ov Day, and I rove at the Secesh lines, when a dirty-looking Confed. called me " Halt," and pinted a bagonet at me. He arst me who I was, an' whar I was gone.

" My friendly ruff," sez I, " I've just bin up North stealin' things an' sich for Jeff. Me an' him air ole pals."

He left me pars.

After travelling a spell, I obsarved a ole house by the road-side, & feelin' faint and thirsty, I entered. The only family I found at home was a likely lookin' young femail gal, whose Johnny had gone for a solger. She was a weepin' bitterly.

" Me putty rose-bud," sez I, " why dost thou weep ? "

She made nary answer, but weepedested on. I placed me hand onto her hed, brusht back the snowy ringlets from her pale brow, an' kis—an' passyfied her.

" What cawsed them tears, fare maid ? " I arskt again.

" Why," sez she, " brother John promist 2 bring me home some Yankee boans to make jewelry, but he had to go an' git killd, & now I won't get ary boan, an'—O, it's 2 bad—boo-hoo-oo-o ! "

Yes, it was muchly 2 bad—and more too. A woman's tears brings the undersined, an' for the time bein' I was a rebel sympathizer.

" Enny fathers ? "

" Only one. But he's dead. Mother went over to see Unkle Reub."

" Was John a putty good brother ? "

" Yes, John was O so kind. His was the only breast I had to repose these weary head onto."

I pitied the maid, and hinted that she might repose her weary head on my shirt front—an' she reposed. And I was her brother John for a while, as it were.

Ere we parted, I arskt for a draught of water to squench me thirst, an' the damsel tript gayly out of the door to pro-cure it. As she was gone a considirable period, I lookt out

the winder and saw her hoppin' briskly 4th, accompanied by
2 secesh cusses, who war armed to the teeth. I begin to
smell as many as two mouses. The "putty dear" had discovered I was a Yankee, an' was goin' to hev me tooken prisoner. I frustrated her plans a few—I leapt out the back
winder as quick as a prestidiguretaterandisch, an' when she
entered the domicil, she found "brother John" non ester
(which is Latin, or sumthin'), and be4 I had proceeded much
I found me timerepeater non ester too. The fare maid, who
was Floyd's Neace, had hookt it while reposin' on me weskit.
It was a hunky watch—a family hair-loom, an' I wouldn't
have parted with it fer a dollar and sixty-nine cents ($1.69).

In doo corse ov mail I arrov in Richmon. I unfolded me
mission, and was ushered into J. Davis's orgust presents.
But the result was not as soothing to weak nerves as my
hart could wish, and I returned to Washington, disgustid
with all peas measures. The sympathizers may do their own
dirt-eatin' in the footer, as they have done in the parst.
Good-by! Adoo! Farewell!

THE AUCTIONEER AND THE LAWYER.

SMITE.

A CITY Auctioneer, one Samuel Stubbs,
    Did greater execution with his hammer,
    Assisted by his puffing clamor,
Than Gog and Magog with their clubs,
Or that great Fee-fa-fum of war.
The Scandinavian Thor,
Did with his mallet, which (see Bryant's
Mythology) fell'd stoutest giants :—
For Samuel knock'd down houses, churches,
And woods of oak and elm and birches,
With greater ease than mad Orlando
Tore the first tree he laid his hand to.

He ought, in reason, to have raised his own
Lot by knocking others' down ;

And had he been content with shaking
His hammer and his hand, and taking
Advantage of what brought him grist, he
Might have been as rich as Christie ;—
But so nehow when thy midnight bell, Bow,
  Sounded along Cheapside its knell,
  Our spark was busy in Pall-mall
Shaking his elbow—
Marking, with paw upon his mazzard,
The turns of hazard ;
Or rattling in a box the dice,
  Which seem'd as if a grudge they bore
To Stubbs ; for often in a trice
Down on the nail he was compell'd to pay
All that his hammer brought him in the day,
  And sometimes more.

Thus, like a male Penelope, our wight,
What he had done by day undid by night;
No wonder, therefore, if like her,
  He was beset by clamorous brutes,
Who crowded round him to prefer
  Their several suits.
One Mr. Snipps, the tailor, had the longest
  Bill for many suits—of raiment,
And naturally thought he had the strongest
  Claim for payment.
But debts of honor must be paid,
Whate'er becomes of debts of trade ;
And so our stylish auctioneer,
From month to month throughout the year,
Excuses, falsehoods, pleas alleges,
Or flatteries, compliments and pledges.
When in the latter mood one day,
He squeez'd his hand, and swore to pay.
" But when ! "   " Next month you may depend on't,
My dearest Snipps, before the end on't ;
Your face proclaims in every feature
You wouldn't harm a fellow-creature—
  You're a kind soul, I know you are, Snipps."

" Ay, so you said six months ago;
But such fine words, I'd have you know,
    Butter no parsnips."
This said, he bade his lawyer draw
    A special writ,
    Serve it on Stubbs, and follow it
Up with the utmost rigor of the law.

This lawyer was a friend of Stubbs;
    That is to say,
    In a civic way,
Where business interposes not its rubs:
For where the main chance is in question,
    Damon leaves Pythias to the stake,
    Pylades and Orestes break,
And Alexander cuts Hephæstion;
But when our man of law *must* sue his friends,
Tenfold politeness makes amends.

So when he meets our Auctioneer,
    Into his outstretch'd hand he thrust his
Writ, and said, with friendly leer,
    " My dear, dear Stubbs, pray do me justice;
In this affair I hope you see
No censure can attach to me—
Don't entertain a wrong impression;
    I'm doing now what must be done
In my profession.''
" And so am I," Stubbs answer'd with a frown;
    So crying " Going—going—going—gone!"
    He knock'd him down!

MR. AND MRS. SKINNER.

HARDWICK.

MR. SKINNER, a respectable middle-aged gentleman, but
of a somewhat convivial turn, was very fond of attending
public dinners, where, as he said, he only went "to support
the chair!" Mrs. Skinner was of a Caudle-like turn of

mind, and was in the habit of cautioning her lord and—no!
not exactly her master, by a few words at parting; such as
"Now mind, dear, don't get worse for the wine," and "Pray
take care of your purse," and "Pray don't stop *after* the
dinner;" to all of which Mr. S. would promise to be particularly attentive, although he would venture upon a mild
remonstrance:

(This is the highly respectable, staid, middle-aged, prudent
Mr. Skinner, *before* going to the dinner.)

"Really, Mrs. Skinner, these remarks are entirely un-
called-for. I should imagine, Mrs. S., that by *this* time you
were fully aware of my strength of mind, and firmness of
resolution. Charity—blessed charity, Mrs. S., prompts me
to go; but rest assured, I shall not give more than what is
necessary to maintain the integrity of my name. I never
allow my heart to get the better of my head, Mrs. Skinner.
If I go to a public dinner, it's as much a matter of business
as pleasure; I never over-do it. Prudence, Mrs. S., prudence is my watchword and motto. I'm not to be betrayed
into over-indulgence, nor late hours; oh, dear, no! *other* men
may have these failings, but *I* have not. My position in society, and well-known respectability, is a sufficient guaran-
tee against anything of that kind. I'm proud—Caroline—
proud, I may say, of my inflexible determination; when I
have once made up my mind, nothing can alter or influence
me; I wouldn't deviate from my fixed purpose, not even for
my own brother, Mrs. S.; you under-value my strength of
mind, and insult me, by supposing me—*me*, Ebenezer Skinner, capable of such vacillation and impropriety. What do
you say? 'Think of the *last* time.' Now, Caroline, you
know the last, as I told you, I was taken suddenly ill, and
was sent to the hospital in a cab, where they detained me
two or three hours; you know I was perfectly sober when I
arrived at home. What do you say? 'That was owing to
the stomach-pump.' Mrs. Skinner, may *you* never be suddenly indisposed at a party. 'The time before that, too, I
didn't come home till morning?' That's too bad, Caroline;

you know perfectly well, the policeman who brought me home told you, as I did myself, that the crowd at the fire was so great I couldn't get through it, and was forced, against my will, into a tavern opposite, where the fumes of the liquors the firemen drank overpowered my finely-strung nerves. But I dare say nothing of that kind will occur to-night, and you may rely upon it, that I shall be guilty of no approach to inebriation—it's what I detest and abhor. Of course I must—like others—respond to the usual loyal toasts ; but beyond that, Mrs. S., don't think, for a moment, I shall go. In fact the truth is, I would rather *not* go at all ; but you see, I am one of the stewards, and *duty*—religious *duty*—Caroline, towards the truly excellent objects of the society, calls upon me, in the sacred name of benevolⱥnce and humanity, to contribute my humble aid to the good cause, and to partake of the annual dinner ; and I cannot, without self-reproach, neglect it ; but, upon the word of a man, who's valued possession is his strength of mind, and power to resist temptation, *I shall be at home by twelve o'clock.* You smile—why so ?—you know my determination of character, Mrs. S., why doubt me ? Mind, I don't say it may not be five minutes *after* twelve, but *not later.* By-the-by, I might as well take a key, and then neither you nor the servant need wait up. You say, 'Oh, no ; you're not going to risk the house being set on fire, with my filthy cigar left burning in the passage again.' Now, Caroline, dearest! that's *not* right ; you know I don't smoke. 'How came it there, then ?' How should I know ? I suppose some one threw it in when I opened the door. However, time presses, it's now nearly five, and I've got to walk to the rank to get a cab ; I must be off. 'I'm to remember that you'll sit up for me ?' Certainly, my dear, prudence and punctuality was always my motto, and punctually at twelve will I be home. Mrs. Skinner—ta-ta."

Mr. Skinner goes to the dinner, and now you will please to suppose he is returning home just as the gray light of daybreak is dawning—somebody has taken (by mistake, of

course) his new silk umbrella and has left him an old ging-
ham—he has lost his own hat, and he has to put up with
one too big for him—he does not go *straight* home, for the
reason that his legs tremble under him and compel him to
walk in a zigzag direction.

(This is the highly respectable, staid, prudent, &c., &c.,
Mr. Skinner, returning home *from* the dinner.)

(*Singing.*) "We're nae that fou, we're nae that fou, but
just a wee drap in our ee." "Why, dear me! dear me!
whatever is the time? Everybody is gone home; I wish *I*
was at home. Here—cab, cab, cab! Why, even all the cabs
are gone home. All the people's gone to bed, except my
wife, *she* ain't, *I* know; she'll wait up for me, to let me in,
instead of the girl—what a fool she *is!* I wish she'd let
Mary Ann sit up to open the door; it would do just as well,
and she wouldn't break her rest. Nice girl, that Mary Ann
—very nice girl. Let me see, let me see; how old's my
wife? Why—forty—forty—ay, forty-four : and she's as
well as ever. Ah! there's no chance *yet!* Now, when I do
get home, I shall catch it—I know I shall; I've given all
the money away, doubled my subscription, and become a
life subscriber. Well, well—'Charity covers a '—what is it?
—(*hiccup*) what is it? 'a multitude of' something. Beautiful song that, the man sung—very touching; something
about 'drying up the Orphan's *Beer!* '—I forget the rest—
cost me five guineas tho'—never mind." (*Singing thickly.*)
" 'Non, Nobis, *Dominoes.*' Non, no, no, no!—hang it, I
don't know; which the deuce is *my* house? I can't see it.
Why (*hiccup*), this isn't *my* street; my street's a terrace,
that goes up steps, with a brass knocker, and a letter-box.
What does it say?—Long—Long—Long Acre! Why, this
ain't the way to Islington Grove!—that's where I live." (*As
if addressing a company.*) "Skinner, gentlemen, will be most
happy and delighted to see you *all* there, gentlemen, come
when you will; Mrs. Skinner will be proud to receive you;
she's a good woman, though I say it; a better creature than
Mrs. S. never breathed, gentlemen; she will make you all

comfortable for a week, if you like, gentlemen." (*Suddenly waking up.*) "Hallo! hallo! What am I talking about? Catch her at it. Why, it was only yesterday she snubbed my city friend, Biffins. She don't like conviv-viv-viv-i-ality, does my wife. I wonder what she'll say to me, being so late? She'll think I've been drinking; she's wrong, though, very wrong! How could I miss my way I can't make out! Why, here's a bridge; I don't go over any bridge to Islington, do I? Certainly not. How the fog gets in one's eyes! I know these fogs will do a deal o' mischief; if it hadn't been for the fog, I should a' been home hours ago—but *she* won't believe it—not a bit of it. She be bothered; she should a' let me have the key; *next* time I *will* have it. (*Hiccup.*) Now I feel as happy as possib-ib-ble. I wonder how people can grumble, and not be charit-a'b-a'b-ble?—they ain't like *me*. Now, there's Bunkins, I'll lend him five pounds to-morrow! And there's Swivell, *his* business is rather shaky; I'll keep him afloat awhile. Then there's Boozle, he asked me to do a bill for twenty, yesterday, and I refused him—how unkind!—I'll do one for fifty, if he likes, in the morning. There's old John, my clerk, too; he's a good old faithful servant; I'll raise his salary directly. Then there's my poor brother Tom, in the work-house. Tom, my boy, you shall come out and be my partner. What a good thing it is to have a kind heart! How I feel for the poor creatures that's badly off! I'll make Mrs. Skinner give away soup in the morning, to all the wretched, starving, poor things that ain't got a bed to eat, and not a bit of bread to lie down upon! I'll fetch in all the ragged boys that tumble after the omnibuses, and clothe 'em, that I will. I'll subscribe to the hospital, for a man don't know what he may come to; and I'll give a poor cabman more than sixpence a mile! I feel for 'em—out in all weathers and all hours." (*With energy.*) "Where are they all? I shan't get home at all! Ah, there's one at last. Here, my man; cab! cab!—home! What do you say? 'Where to?' Why, home—Islington Grove;—drive on, and charge what you like. Mrs. Skinner

must pay it. Won't she like *that?* Well, never mind, I
shall sleep like a top while she talks. I'm all right now I've
got a cab—in I go!" (*Singing.*) "'Old Simon the Cellarer
keeps a—a'—oh, I don't know; that's what the man sung.
All right, cabby, I'm ready; help me in, old boy; here's a
cigar, and drive on!"

THE BACHELOR AND THE BRIDE.

ANONYMOUS.

FRANK FORETHOUGHT was a very careful fellow,
    In all his actions circumspect and wise;
Never quite fuddled, very seldom mellow,
    Nor e'er for love heaved unavailing sighs;
For glances which all other hearts could gain,
On him bestow'd, were still bestow'd in vain.

And let not lovesick youths, with upcast eyes,
    Nor reeling sots, or let such only blame;
To those who liberty and reason prize,
    To be in love or liquor is the same:
Such follies we in either case commit,
As are for fools or madmen only fit.

Frank, though near forty, had (the observation
    I made just now) both love and wine defied,
When, all at once, he felt a strange sensation—
    A sort of throbbing at his larboard side
(As sailors term it), with a sudden flush,
As if the blood forth from his frame would rush.

His pulse, before so temperate, now grew quick,
    And sighs (unknown before) he scarce could smother,
So as he felt inclining to be sick
    He took a dram, another, and another: .
This plan, though oft the best, as matters stood,
In his dilemma, did more harm than good.

What, in the sufferer, caused this state alarming
 Scarce need I say ; what but a woman could ?
And this was young and fair, resolved on charming ;
 And though he lon_ her blandishments withstood,
Oft on her eyes incautious would he gaze,
Until at last they set him in a blaze

Those eyes so fatal were to all beholders,
 Like gas, at once could light and heat impart :
I'd have a score of hazels at my shoulders,
 Rather then two such hazels at my heart.
When glowing glances of fond feelings tell us,
How thrills—but stop, I mustn't make spouse jealous.

So to proceed, our swain was like a tree,
 Which sapless grown is easier made to flame ;
This fair assailant plied most dexterously
 Her smiles and wiles, till quite secured her aim ;
And these attacks, in ardor unabated,
Had brought him to the state before related.

He thought of naught but her who'd caused his pain
 Sleeping or waking, and the charm grew stronger ;
Therefore resolved, since struggling was in vain,
 To marry—and to think of her no longer :
She, press'd to name the day, could scarcely speak,
But blushing, sighing, murmur'd "Sunday week."

Frank had a mother, whom he much respected
 (For she'd a fortune at her own disposal),
And much he fear'd that if by her detected
 In marriage project, hopes of wealth would close all,
Since she had vow'd, if he inclined to wed,
To lead a second husband to her bed.

And it so chanced there was a strolling player
 To whom she seem'd a willing ear to lend ;
Frank knew not this—and yet with secret care
 Procured a ring, a license, and a friend
Who would act as father to his destined bride,
And keep the secret from the world beside.

The time arrived, and Forethought, with his friend,
   Might snugly station'd in the porch be seen,
Expecting that the bride would thither bend
   Her course; she came not—with impatience keen
The kind companion would no longer stay,
But went to know the cause of this delay

I once was angling, and with great delight
   Hook'd several fish, felt of my skill much vanity,
But when I couldn't get another bite,
   Began to feel a vast deal of humanity;
And 'gainst the barbarous sport my anger rising,
Put up and went away philosophizing.

In this state were Frank's feelings: he began
   To think 'twould prove a fortunate miscarriage,
And that for him, perhaps, the wisest plan
   Was to go home, and think no more of marriage.
But while these thoughts in his suspense oppress'd him,
A man of smart appearance thus address'd him.

" Sir, I came here hoping to wed in private—
   I wish'd to keep some persons in the dark,
So meant, lest they the knowledge should arrive at,
   To take my mate from no one but the clerk;
Since he refuses, I make free to ask,
If you in kindness will perform the task.

" But for a few short moments 'twill detain you,
   The minister and bride are waiting there."
Says Frank, " By a refusal I'll not pain you,
   Though 'pon my word this is a strange affair;
I meant to take a wife myself to-day!
And never dreamt of giving one away!"

The clergyman look'd grave—the knot was tied—
   The fees were paid; his smiles were then benign;
With curious eye our hero view'd the bride,
   But still she hid her countenance divine;

And e'en her natural tones contrived to smother;
At length he caught a glimpse, and—'twas his mother!

The rest is plain—she who had Frank decoy'd,
　　Was sister to this fortune-hunting swain:
Who had her fascinating arts employ'd,
　　To banish any scruples might remain,
Her son respecting, in the matron's mind,
By proving him to wedlock's joys inclined.

Now all you single gentlemen of forty,
　　Take warning by Frank Forethought's piteous case;
How happy I should this, my tale, have taught ye,
　　By his example to avoid disgrace.
Moist spring, and glowing summer, having past,
Do not in autumn catch love's plague at last.

THE DRUNKARD AND HIS WIFE.

LA FONTAINE.

EACH one's his faults, to which he still holds fast,
　　And neither shame nor fear can cure the man;
　　'Tis *apropros* of this (my usual plan),
I give a story, for example, from the past.
　　A follower of Bacchus hurt his purse,
　　His health, his mind, and still grew each day worse;
　　Such people, ere they're run one-half their course,
Drain all their fortune for their mad expenses.
　　One day this fellow, by the wine o'erthrown,
Had in a bottle left his senses;
　　His shrewd wife shut him all alone
In a dark tomb, till the dull fume
　　Might from his brains evaporate.
He woke and found the place all gloom,
　　A shroud upon him cold and damp,
　　Upon the pall a funeral lamp.
"What's this?" said he, "my wife's a widow, then!"
　　On that the wife, dressed like a Fury, came.

Mask'd and with voice disguised, into the den,
　And brought the wretched sot, in hopes to tame,
Some boiling gruel fit for Lucifer.
　The sot no longer doubted he was dead—
A citizen of Pluto's—could he err?
　"And who are you?" unto the ghost he said.
"I'm Satan's steward," said the wife, "and serve the food
　For those within this black and dismal place."
　The sot replied, with comical grimace,
Not taking any time to think,
"And don't you also bring the drink?"

A WESTERN LAWYER'S PLEA AGAINST THE FACT.

GENTLEMEN OF THE JURY:—The Scripture saith, "Thou shalt not kill;" now, if you hang my client, you transgress the command as slick as grease, and as plump as a goose egg in a loafer's face. Gentlemen, murder is murder, whether committed by twelve jurymen, or by a humble individual like my client. Gentlemen, I do not deny the fact of my client having killed a man, but is that any reason why you should do so? No such thing, gentlemen; you may bring the prisoner in "guilty;" the hangman may do his duty; but will that exonerate you? No such thing; in that case you will be murderers. Who among you is prepared for the brand of Cain to be stamped upon his brow to-day? Who, freemen—who in this land of liberty and light? Gentlemen, I will pledge my word, not one of you has a bowie-knife or a pistol in his pocket. No, gentlemen, your pockets are odoriferous with the perfumes of cigar cases and tobacco. You can smoke the pipe of a peaceful conscience; but hang my unfortunate client, and the scaly alligators of remorse will gallop through the internal principles of animal viscera, until the spinal vertebræ of your anatomical construction is turned into a railroad, for the grim and gory goblins of despair. Gentlemen, beware of committing murder! Beware, I say, of meddling with the eternal prerogative! Gentlemen, I adjure you, by the manumitted ghost of temporal sanctity, to do no murder.   I adjure you, by the name of woman, the mainspring of the tickling timepiece of time's theoretical transmigration, to do no murder!   I adjure you, by the love you have for the esculent and condimental gusto of our native pumpkin, to do no murder!   I adjure you, by the stars set in the flying ensign of your emancipated country, to do no murder!   I adjure you, by the American Eagle that whipped the universal game cock of creation, and now sits roosting on the magnetic telegraph of time's illustrious transmigration, do no murder!   And lastly, gentlemen, if you ever expect to wear store-made coats—if you ever expect to wear boots made of the free hide of the Rocky Mountain buffalo—and, to sum up all, if you ever expect to be anything but a set of sneaking, loafing, rascally, cut-throated, braided small ends of humanity, whittled down into indistinctibility, acquit my client, and save your country.

The prisoner was acquitted.

READING A TRAGEDY.
BAYLY.

OH, proud am I, exceeding proud, I've mustered the *Elite !*
I'll read them my new Tragedy—no ordinary treat ;
It has a deeply-stirring plot—the moment I commence
They'll feel for my sweet heroine an interest intense ;
It never lags, it never flags, it cannot fail to touch ;
Indeed, I fear the sensitive may feel it *over* much ;
But still a dash of pathos with my terrors I combine,
The bright reward of tragic bard—the laurel will be mine !

Place chairs for all the company, and, ma'am, I really think
If you don't send that child to bed, he will not sleep a wink ;
I know he'll screech like anything before I've read a page ·
My second act would terrify a creature of that age ;
And should the darling, scared by me, become an *imbecile*,
Though *flatter'd* at the circumstance—how sorry I should feel !

What! *won't* you send the child to bed? well, madam, we shall see;
Pray take a chair, and now prepare the laurel crown for me.

Have *all* got pocket handkerchiefs? your tears will fall in streams:
Place water near to sprinkle over any one who screams;
And pray, good people, recollect, when what I've said controls
Your sympathies, and actually harrows up your souls,
Remember (it may save you all from suicide or fits),
'Tis but a mortal man who but opes the floodgates of his wits;
Retain your intellects to trace my brightest gem (*my moral*),
And, when I've done, I'm *very* sure you'll wreathe my brow with
    laurel.

Hem—"*Act the First, and Scene the First—A Wood—Bumrumpti
    enters—*
Bumrumpti speaks, 'And have I then escaped from my tormentors?
Revenge! revenge! oh, were they dead, and *I* a carrion crow,
I'd pick the flesh from off their bones, I'd sever toe from toe!
Shall fair Fryfitta, pledged to me, her plighted vow recall,
And wed with hated Snookums or with *any* man at all!
No—rather perish earth and sea, the sky and—all the rest of it—
For wife to me she swore she'd be, and she *must* make the best of it.'"

Through five long acts—ay, *very* long—the happy bard proceeds;
Without a pause, without applause, scene after scene he reads!
That *silent* homage glads his heart! it silent well may be;
Not one of all his slumbering friends can either hear or see!
The anxious chaperon is asleep! the beau beside the fair!
The dog is sleeping on the rug! the cat upon the chair!
Old men and babes—the footman, too! oh, if we crown the bard
We'll twine for him the *poppy* wreath, his only fit reward.

CAST-OFF GARMENTS.

From "Nothing to Wear."

BUTLER.

WELL, having thus wooed Miss M'Flimsey and gained her,
With the silks, crinolines and hoops that contained her,
I had, as I thought, a contingent remainder
At least in the property, and the best right

To appear as its escort by day and by night:
And it being the week of the Stuckups' grand ball—
    Their cards had been out for a fortnight or so,
    And set the Avenue on the tiptoe—
I considered it only my duty to call,
    And see if Miss Flora intended to go.
I found her—as ladies are apt to be found,
When the time intervening between the first sound
Of the bell and the visitor's entry is shorter
Than usual—I found; I won't say—I caught her—
Intent on the pier-glass, undoubtedly meaning
To see if perhaps it didn't need cleaning.
She turned as I entered—" Why, Harry, you sinner,
I thought that you went to the Flashers' to dinner ! "
" So I did," I replied, " but the dinner is swallowed,
    And digested, I trust, for 'tis now nine and more;
So being relieved from that duty, I followed
    Inclination, which led me, you see, to your door.
And now will your ladyship so condescend
As just to inform me if you intend
Your beauty, and graces, and presence to lend
(All which, when I own, I hope no one will borrow),
To the Stuckups', whose party, you know, is to-morrow ?
The fair Flora looked up with a pitiful air,
And answered quite promptly, " Why, Harry, mon cher,
I should like above all things to go with you there;
But really and truly—I've nothing to wear.''
" Nothing to wear ! go just as you are;
Wear the dress you have on, and you'll be by far,
I engage, the most bright and particular star
    On the Stuckup horizon "—I stopped, for her eye,
Notwithstanding this delicate onset of flattery,
Opened on me at once a most terrible battery
    Of scorn and amazement.   She made no reply,
But gave a slight turn to the end of her nose
    (That pure Grecian feature), as much as to say,
" How absurd that any sane man should suppose
That a lady would go to a ball in the clothes,
    No matter how fine, that she wears every day ! "

So I ventured again—" Wear your crimson brocade,"
(Second turn up of nose)—" That's too dark by a shade."
" Your blue silk "—" That's too heavy ; " " Your pink "—
    " That's too light."
" Wear tulle over satin "—" I can't endure white."
" Your rose-colored, then, the best of the batch "—
" I haven't a thread of point lace to match."
" Your brown moire antique "—" Yes, and look like a Quaker ; "
" The pearl-colored "—' I would, but that plaguey dressmaker
Has had it a week "—" Then that exquisite lilac,
In which you would melt the heart of a Shylock."
(Here the nose took again the same elevation.)
" I wouldn't wear that for the whole of creation."
    " Why not ? It's my fancy, there's nothing could strike it,
As more *comme il faut* "—" Yes, but dear me, that lean
    Sophronia Stuckup has got one just like it,
And I won't appear dressed like a chit of sixteen."
" Then that splendid purple, that sweet Mazarine ;
That superb point d'aiguille, that imperial green,
That zephyr-like tarletan, that rich grenadine "—
" Not one of all which is fit to b seen,"
Said the lady, becoming excited and flushed.
" Then wear," I exclaimed, in a tone which quite crushed
    Opposition, " that gorgeous toilet which you sported
In Paris last spring, at the grand presentation,
When you quite turned the head of the head of the nation,
    And by all the grand court were so very much courted."
    The end of the nose was portentously tipped up,
And both the bright eyes shot forth indignation,
As she burst upon me with the fierce exclamation,
" I have worn it three times at the least calculation,
And that, and the most of my dresses are ripped up ! "
Here *I ripped out* something, perhaps rather rash.

    Quite innocent though ; but to use an expression
More striking than classic, " it settled my hash,"
    And proved very soon the last act of our session
" Fiddlesticks, is it, sir ? I wonder the ceiling
Doesn't fall down and crush you—oh, you men have no feeling
You selfish, unnatural, illiberal creatures,

Who set yourselves up as patterns and preachers.
Your silly pretence—why what a mere guess it is!
Pray, what do you know of woman's necessities?
I have told you and shown you I've nothing to wear,
And it's perfectly plain you not only don't care,
But you do not believe me" (here the nose went still higher).
" I suppose if you dared you would call me a liar.
Our engagement is ended, sir—yes, on the spot;
You're a brute, and a monster, and—I don't know what."
I mildly suggested the words—Hottentot,
Pickpocket, and cannibal, Tartar, and thief,
As gentle expletives which might give relief;
But this only proved as spark to the powder,
And the storm I had raised came faster and louder;
It blew and it rained, thundered, lightened and hailed
Interjections, verbs, pronouns, till language quite failed
To express the abusive, and then its arrears
Were brought up all at once by a torrent of tears,
And my last faint, despairing attempt at an obs-
Ervation was lost in a tempest of sobs.

HOW TO CURE A COUGH.

ANONYMOUS

ONE Biddy Brown, a country dame,
 As 'tis by many told,
Went to a doctor—Drench by name—
 For she had caught a cold.

And sad, indeed, was Biddy's pain,
 The truth must be confest,
Which she to ease found all in vain,
 For it was at her chest.

The doctor heard her case—and then,
 Determined to assist her,
Prescribed—oh! tenderest of men,
 Upon her *chest* a blister!

Away went Biddy, and next day
   She called on Drench again.
" Well, have you used the blister, pray·
   And has it eased your pain ? "

" Ay, zur," the dame, with curtsey cries,
   " Indeed, I never mocks ;
But, bless ye ! I'd no *chest* the size,
   So I put it on a *box*.

" But, la ! zur, it be little use,
   It never *rose* a bit ;
And you may see it if you choose,
   For there it's sticking yet ! "

THE SOLDIER'S RETURN.

AN ETHIOPIAN DIALOGUE.

WHITE.

SCENE.—*A Wood.*

Enter OLD SOLDIER, R., *with valise, and in old black coat, large shoes, &c.*

SOLDIER. Dis must be de place; ebery tree and shrub
am familiar to me—eben de ole pump dat I passed just now
has a 'semblance ob days gone by. It seems to me a·—
a——

   Enter GEORGE, L., *with whitewash pan and brush.*

Ah ! here comes some one dat can gib me de information I
seek. Young man, can you tell me if—ah ! for three weeks
I have not tasted food.

GEORGE. (*Aside.*) He must be rather peckish by dis time!

SOLDIER. Twenty years ago I left dis spot, an' my poor
little bruder must be quite a man by dis time. I left him
gambolling on de hillside.

GEORGE. (*Aside.*) Oh ! he was a gambler. Oh my ! (SOL-
DIER *advances*, R., *and drops valise on* GEORGE'S *toes.*) Oh dear !

SOLDIER. Ha ! wouldst rob me of my all? (*Seizes him.*)

GEORGE. Oh don't ! I wouldn't take nuffin.

SOLDIER. My all is in dat casket.

GEORGE. His *awl!* Why, he must be a shoemaker. Say, hab you got your lapstone an' hammer wid you?

SOLDIER. (*Looking around.*) I haven't seen an honest face since I came into dis part ob de country. I really a—(To TOM, *sitting.*) Well, there is one; dat's what I called a good, honest, open countenance.

GEORGE. Yes, you'd say so if you could only see him about dinner time.

SOLDIER. Young man! (*Advances.*) Wouldst listen to a painful story?

GEORGE. I would for twenty years.

SOLDIER. Twenty years! Listen then, an' mark me. (GEORGE *marks him on the back with whitewash brush.*) Twenty years ago—do I live while I tell it?—(*weeps*) there lived in dis village a respectful colored woman who had two sons, both boys.

GEORGE. Both boys! Wasn't one ob dem a gal?

SOLDIER. Silence and listen. For many years dey grew up, de delight of dere parents, till the oldest boy conceived de idea ob joining de army. De ole folks interfered to make him change his mind, but go he would; so dere was no use in talkin'. He left dere side in de summer bloom, an' in one hour—one short hour—he was thousands an' thousands ob miles away. Since dat day, he has neber seen his aged sire, an 'longs for de time when he shall see once more dat little gambolling bruder, on de hillside—

GEORGE. Does my ears deceibe my *eyesight?* Ah! (*Looks at his feet, his shoes, &c.*) Had you a muder?

SOLDIER. I *had* a muder. Why, ob coarse I had a muder.

GEORGE. Dat muder had two sons—boys?

SOLDIER. She had, as you remark.

GEORGE. One day, he left for parts unknown; he has neber been heaid ob since dat day.

> "An' one dreadful night the wind it blew,
>   De thunder thundered and de snow it snew!"

SOLDIER. Hum! (*Both approach in front.*)

GEORGE. Ha! ha! he! ho! hu! hy! Methinks I should know dat bruder by a scar on his wrist.

SOLDIER. I hab dat scar, an' many a good ole soldier hab I scar'd wid it.

GEORGE. Dat eyes!

SOLDIER. Dem nose!

GEORGE. Dose har!

SOLDEIR. Dat feet! Oh dear! Twelve at least!

BOTH. Ha! ha! ha! ha! ha! ha! ha! ha! Come to de arms of your long-losted bruder! (*Both fall awkwardly—* GEORGE *gets up very sulky.*)

GEORGE. I don't care to meet any more ob my relations just about now; no, siree! (*Limps off,* L.)

SOLDIER. Stop little bruder George, and listen to de rest ob my misfortunes and history for twenty years. (*Hobbles after him.*)

THE COUNTRYMEN AND THE ASS.

BYROM.

A COUNTRY fellow and his son, they tell
In modern fables, had an ass to sell:
For this intent they turned it out to play,
And fed so well, that by the destined day,
They brought the creature into sleek repair,
And drove it gently to a neighboring fair.

As they were jogging on, a rural class
Was heard to say, " Look! look there, at that ass!
And those two blockheads trudging on each side,
That have not, either of 'em, sense to ride;
Asses all three!" And thus the country folks
On man and boy began to cut their jokes.

Th' old fellow minded nothing that they said,
But every word stuck in the young one's head;
And thus began their comment thereupon:
" Ne'er heed 'm, lad." " Nay, father, do get on."

"Not I, indeed." "Why, then, let me, I pray."
"Well, do ; and see what prating tongues will **say**."

The boy was mounted ; and they had not got
Much further on, before another knot,
Just as the ass was pacing by, pad, pad,
Cried, " O ! that lazy looby of a lad !
How unconcernedly the gaping brute
Lets the poor aged fellow walk a-foot."

Down came the son, on hearing this account,
And begged and prayed, and made his father mount ;
Till a third party, on a further stretch,
" See ! see " exclaimed, "that old hard-hearted wretch !
How like a justice there he sits, or squire ;
While the poor lad keeps wading through the mire."

" Stop," cried the lad, still vexed in deeper mind,
" Stop, father, stop ; let me get on behind."
This done, they thought they certainly should p!ease,
Escape reproaches, and be both at ease ;
For, having tried each practicable way,
What could be left for jokers now to say ?

Still disappointed by succeeding tone,
" Hark ye, you fellows ! Is that ass your own ?
Get off, for shame ! or one of you, at least !
You both deserve to carry the poor beast,
Ready to drop down dead upon the road,
With such a huge unconscionable load."

On this they both dismounted ; and, some say,
Contrived to carry, like a truss of hay,
The ass between 'em ; prints, they add, are **seen**
With man and lad, and slinging ass between;
Others omit that fancy in the print,
As overstraining an ingenious hint.

The copy that we follow says, the man
Rubbed down the ass, and took to his first plan,

Walked to the fair, and sold him, got his price,
  And gave his son this pertinent advice:
"Let talkers talk ; stick thou to what is best;
  To think of pleasing all—is all a jest."

COME AND GO.

SHARPE.

Dick Dawdle had land worth two hundred a-year,
  Yet from debt and from dunning he never was free,
His intellect was not surprisingly clear,
  But he never felt satisfied how it could be.

The raps at his door, and the rings at his gate,
  And the threats of a jail he no longer could bear;
So he made up his mind to sell half his estate,
  Which would pay all his debts, and leave something to spare

He leased to a farmer the rest of his land
  For twenty-one years ; and on each quarter day
The honest man went with the rent in his hand,
  His liberal landlord, delighted, to pay.

Before half the term of the lease had expired,
  The farmer, one day, with a bagful of gold,
Said, " Pardon me, sir, but I long have desired
  To purchase my farm, if the land can be sold.

" Ten years I've been blest with success and with health,
  With trials a few—I thank God, not severe—
I am grateful, I hope, though not proud of my wealth,
  But I've managed to lay by a hundred a year."

" Why how," exclaimed Dick, " can this possibly be ? "
  (With a stare of surprise, and a mortified laugh);
" The *whole* of my farm proved too little for *me*,
  And *you*, it appears, have grown rich upon *half*."

" I hope you'll excuse me," the farmer replies,
  " But I'll tell you the cause, if your honor would know;

In two little words all the difference lies,
   I always say *come*, and you used to say *go*."

" Well, and what does that mean, my good fellow ? " he said.
   " Why this, sir, that *I* always rise with the sun ;
You said ' *go* ' to your man, as you lay in your bed,
   I say, ' *Come*, Jack, with me,' and I see the work done."

HOW THEY POP THE QUESTION.

ANONYMOUS.

THE sailor says : " I like your rig ;
   And though I've noticed many,
I really think you are, old girl,
   As trim a craft as any.
And if you'll say the word,
   Through every kind of weather,
Just blast my timbers if we don't
   Go cruising on together."

The poet with enraptured gaze,
   Points out a single star—
" 'Tis thus, sweet lady, that you shine
   On mortals from afar ;
But ah ! it is my fondest hope—
   Though selfish, I must own—
That in some modest, vine-wreathed cot
   You'll shine for me alone."

The dancing master—French, of course—
   Thinks earnestly of mating,
And seeks some lovely widow with
   A bow excruciating.
" Madame, ze heart is in ze hope
   You love a leetle beet,
And go ze way of life wiz me—
   Madame, I kees your feet."

The actor quotes from many plays,
　And swears by all the powers,
His hand shall build his Annabelle
　A cot among the flowers.
Without her smiles he e'er is like
　A ship without a rudder ;
Then talks of dark despair and death,
　Until he makes her shudder.

And Pat, the coachman, winks at Bid,
　As she flies from room to room—
The ever merry chambermaid,
　With dusting-pan and broom—
He says, " Me darlint, when we've laid
　Us by a heap of money,
We'll get the praste to tie the knot,
　If you'll say yes, me honey."

Says Hans Von Schmidt, who keeps saloon,
　" I want to get un vrow,
As helps me make der lager pier,
　Und milks de prindle cow ;
To make mine shirts, und cook der krout,
　Und eberytings to do ;
To feed der horse und slop der pig,
　Und tend my papies too."

And even Sam, the barber-man,
　At Lize rolls up his eyes,
And talks of matrimonial bliss,
　With most heart-rending sighs.
" Ef you don't gub dat lily hand
　To dis yer lub-sick nigger,
He puts dis pistol to him head,
　And den he pulls the trigger."

'Tis thus mankind rush to their fate,
　For with a brilliant light,
That little elfin being, Love,

Has power beyond the sight.
Like children's barks, adown the falls,
  To waters still below,
Some glide along without a heart,
  And some to ruin go.

THE CLEVER IDIOT.

ANONYMOUS

A BOY, as nursery records tell,
Had dropp'd his drumstick in a well;
He had good sense enough to know
He would be beaten for't, and so
Slily (tho' silly from his cradle)
Took from the shelf a silver ladle,
And in the water down it goes,
After the drumstick, I suppose.

The thing was miss'd, the servants blamed,
But in a week no longer named;
Now this not suiting his designs,
A silver cup he next purloins
(To aid his plan, he never stopp'd),
And in the water down it dropped.

This caused some words and much inquiry,
And made his parents rather *iry;*
Both for a week were vex'd and cross,
And then—submitted to the loss.
At length, to follow up his plan,
Our little, clever idiot man,
His father's favorite silver waiter
Next cast into the wat'ry crater.

Now this, indeed, was what the cook
And butler could not overlook;
And all the servants of the place
Were searched, and held in much disgrace.

The boy now call'd out, " Cook, here—Nell ;
What's this so shining in the well ? "

This was enough to give a hint
That the lost treasure might be in't ;
So for a man with speed they sent,
Who down the well directly went.
They listen with expectant ear,
At last these joyful words they hear,
" Oh, here's the ladle, and the cup,
And waiter too—so draw me up."

" Hold (quoth the boy), a moment stay,
Bring something else that's in your way."
Adding (with self-approving grin),
" My drumstick, now your hand is in."

THE KNIGHTS; OR, BOTH RIGHT AND BOTH WRONG.

WHEN chivalry was all the taste,
And honor stamped each dauntless breast ;
When falsehood was esteemed a shame,
And heroes bled for virtuous fame ;
To right the wronged, protect the weak,
And dry the tear on beauty's cheek ;
Two bearded knights, on milk-white steeds,
Equipped for tilts, and martial deeds,
Perchance met on a spacious plain,
Where stood a trophy to the slain ;
A mighty shield, on one side white,
The other black as ebon night ;
Emblem of spotless virtue's fall,
And death's dark triumph over all.

Both stopped to view this curious sight,
But viewed it in a different light:

" Bless me ! " cries one, how white this shield !
How bright it shines across the field ! "
" White ! " says the other, " no such thing ;
'Tis blacker than the raven's wing ! "
" Recall your words, presumptuous youth ;
A knight should never jest with truth."
" 'Tis you who want to jest, not I.
The shield is black ! "   " By heaven, you lie ! "
" Now, Truth, bear witness to my vow—
I'll die, base knight, or make thee bow ! "
While both with sudden passion stormed,
And rage each angry face deformed,
From wordy war, to blows they turn,
And with revenge and fury burn :
On either helm the sword descends,
Each trusty helm the head defends ;
And on the impenetrable mail,
The sounding strokes fall thick as hail.
They prance their coursers round and round,
Each hopes to give the lucky wound ;
And each, convinced himself is right,
Maintains, with equal hope, the fight;
Nor doubts to make his rival own,
Success attends on truth alone.

By chance, a clown, who passed that way,
At a distance saw the doubtful fray ;
Who, though he relished not hard blows,
Esteemed it right to interpose.

" Good sirs ! " he cried, then made his bow,
Respectful, diffident and low,
" I'm but a simple man, 'tis true !
But wish to serve and save you too ;
And he who's wronged, I'll take his part,
With all my soul, and all my heart ! "

The knights, by this time almost spent,
To honest Hodge attention lent :

For e'en the presence of a fool
Will sometimes stubborn stomachs cool;
And when for trifles men fall out
A trifle oft brings peace about.

Each, thinking Hodge must prove him right,
And justify his partial sight,
Made haste the matter to disclose,
That caused this war of words and blows,
And asked if black or white the shield,
That stood conspicuous on the field,
For passion still had kept them blind;
Passion, the shutters of the mind.
"Faith," said the clown, and scratched his head,
"Your honors straight shall be obeyed:
'Tis neither white nor black, but both ·
And this is true I ll take my oath.
One side is black, the other white:
Each saw it in a single light,
But had you viewed the shield all round,
Both would have right and wrong been found.

The wondering knights like stuck pigs stared,
While Hodge the simple truth declared;
And each, ashamed of passion's sway,
Lifts up his eyes; when, bright as day,
The shield both black and white appeared,
And both from falsehood's stain were cleared.
They thanked kind Hodge, and parted friends;
Resolved for wrath to make amends,
By looking twice ere once they fought,
And always aiding strength with thought.

Hence we this precious moral draw;
Fixed as the Medes and Persians' law—
That he who only one side sees,
With erring judgment oft decrees;
And he who only one tale hears,
'Gainst half the truth oft shuts his ears.

HOW THE LAWYER GOT A PATRON SAINT.

A LEGEND OF BRETAGNE.

SAXE.

A LAWYER of Brittany, once on a time,
  When business was flagging at home,
Was sent as a legate to Italy's clime,
  To confer with the Father at Rome.

And what was the message the minister brought ?
  To the Pope he preferred a complaint
That each other profession a Patron had got,
  While the Lawyers had never a Saint!

"Very true," said his Holiness,—smiling to find
  An attorney so civil and pleasant,—
"But my very last Saint is already assigned,
  And I can't make a new one at present.

"To choose from the *Bar* it were fittest, I think ;
  Perhaps you've a man in your eye ;"
And his Holiness here gave a mischievous wink
  To a Cardinal sitting near by.

But the lawyer replied, in a lawyer-like way,
  " I know what is modest, I hope ;
I didn't come hither, allow me to say
  To proffer advice to the Pope ! "

"Very well," said his Holiness, "then we will do
  The best that may fairly be done ;
It don't seem exactly the thing, it is true,
  That the Law should be Saint-less alone.

"To treat your profession as well as I can,
  And leave you no cause of complaint,
I propose, as the only quite feasible plan,
  To give you a second-hand Saint.

"To the neighboring church you will presently go
   And this is the plan I advise :—
First, say a few *aves*—a hundred or so—
   Then, carefully bandage your eyes;

"Then (saying more *aves*) go groping around,
   And, touching one object alone,
The Saint you are seeking will quickly be found,
   For the first that you touch is your own."

The lawyer did as his Holiness said,
   Without an omission or flaw;
Then, taking the bandages off from his head,
   What do you think he saw?

There was St. Michael (figured in paint)
   Subduing the Father of Evil;
And the lawyer, exclaiming "Be *thou* our Saint!"
   Was touching the form of the DEVIL!

JOSH BILLINGS ON LAUGHING.

LAUGHING is strikly an amuzement, altho some folks make
a bizzness ov it. It haz bin considered an index ov karakter,
and thare iz sum, so close at reasoning, that they say, they
kan tell what a man had for dinner, by seeing him laff. I
never saw two laff alike. While thare are some, who don't
make enny noise, thare are sum, who dont make ennything
but noise; and some agin, who hav musik in their laff, and
others, who laff just az a rat duz, who haz caught a steel
trap with his tale. Thare is no mistake in the assershun,
that it is a cumfert tew hear sum laffs, that cum rompin out
ov a man's mouth, just like a distrik school ov yung girls
let out tew play. Then agin thare iz sum laffs, that are az
kold and meaningless az a yesterday's bukwheat pancake—
that cum out ov the mouth twisted, and gritty, az a 2 inch
auger, drawed out ov a hemlok board. One ov these kind

ov laffs haz no more cumfert in it than the—stummuk ake
haz, and makes yu feel, when yu hear it, az though yu waz
being shaved bi a dull razer, without the benefit ov soap,
or klergy.   Men who never laff may have good hartes,
but they are deep seated—like sum springs, they hav their
inlet and outlet from below, and show no sparkling bubble
on the brim.   I dont like a gigler, this kind ov laff iz like
the dandylion, a feeble yeller, and not a bit ov good smell
about it.   It iz true that enny kind ov a laff iz better than
none—but giv me the laff that looks out ov a man's eyes
fust, to see if the coast is clear, then steals down into the
dimple ov his cheek, and rides in an eddy thare awhile,
then waltzes a spell, at the korners ov his mouth, like a
thing ov life, then busts its bonds ov buty, and fills the air
for a moment with a shower ov silvery tongued sparks—
then steals bak, with a smile, to its lair, in the harte, tew
watch agin for its prey—this it is the kind ov laff that i luv
and ain't afrade ov.

THE NIGHT AFTER CHRISTMAS.

ANONYMOUS.

'Twas the night *after* Christmas—when all through the house
Every soul was abed, and as still as a mouse,
Those stockings, so lately St. Nicholas' care,
We:e emptied of all that was eatable there.
The darlings had duly been tucked in their beds,
With very full stomachs, and pain in their heads ;
I was dozing away in my new cotton cap,
And Nancy was rather far gone in a nap,
When out in the nurs'ry arose such a clatter,
I sprang from my sleep, crying " What is the matter ? "
I rushed to each bedside, still half in a doze,
Tore open the curtains, and threw down the clothes,
While the light of the taper served clearly to show
The piteous plight of those objects below.
For what to the fond father's eyes should appear,
But the little pale face of each sick little dear.

Each pet, having crammed itself full as a tick,
I knew in a moment now felt like " Old Nick."
Their pulses were rapid, their breathings the same,
What their stomachs rejected I'll mention by name :
Now turkey, now stuffing, plum-pudding—of course
Now custards, now·comfits, now cranberry sauce :
Before outraged nature each went to the wall,
Aye ! lollypops, flapdoddle—great things and small,
As from throes epigastric, indigestibles fly,
So figs, nuts and raisins, jam, jelly and pie :
All the horrors of surfeit thus brought to my view,
To the shame of mamma and Santa Claus too.
I turned from the sight : to my bed-room stepped back,
And brought out a vial marked "Pulv. Ipecac,"
When my Nancy exclaimed (for their sufferings shocked her),
" Don't you think you had better, love, run for the doctor ? "
I ran—and was scarcely back under the roof,
When I heard the sharp clatter of old Jalap's hoof ;
I might say—I had hardly had time to turn 'round,
When the doctor came into the room with a bound.
He was spattered with mud from his hat to his boots,
And the clothes he had on seemed the drollest of suits ;
In his haste he'd put all quite awry on his back,
And he looked like John Falstaff half-fuddled with sack.
His eyes how they twinkled ! Had the doctor got merry ?
His cheeks looked like Port, and his breath smelt of Sherry ;
Ie hadn't been shaved—so to baffle the breeze,
The beard on his chin served as " *cheveux de frise.*"
But inspecting their tongues in despite of their teeth,
And drawing his watch from his waistcoat beneath,
He felt of each pulse, saying " each little belly
Must get rid of the rest of that pie-crust and jelly."
I gazed on each chubby, plump, sick little elf,
And groaned when he said it, in spite of myself ;
But a wink of his eye, as he physicked dear Fred,
Soon gave me to know I had nothing to dread ;
He didn't prescribe—but went straightway to work
And dosed all the rest—gave his trousers a jerk,
And adding directions while blowing his nose,

He buttoned his coat—from his chair he arose,
Then jumped in his gig—gave old Jalap a whistle,
And Jalap dashed off as if pricked by a thistle ;
But the doctor exclaimed ere he drove out of sight,
" More cases just like them ! Good night ! Jones, good night ! "

A CHANGE OF SYSTEM.

A PETITE COMEDY IN ONE ACT.

HOWARD PAUL.

Characters.

SIR CHARLES RIPPLE, BART.
LYTTLETON PAGE, ESQ.
MRS. DARLINGTON.

COSTUMES—*Ordinary, of the day.*

STAGE DIRECTIONS.—*R. means Right ; L., Left ; C., Centre; R. C., Right of Centre ; L. C., Left of Centre ; D. F., Door in the Flat, or Scene running across the back of the Stage ; C. D. F., Centre Door in the Flat ; D. R. C., Right Door in the Flat ; L. C. F., Left Door in the Flat ; R. D., Right Door ; L. D., Left Door ; 2 E., Second Entrance ; U. E., Upper Entrance. The reader is supposed to be on the Stage, facing the audience.*

SCENE.—*A drawing-room elegantly furnished. Door C. and R. and L. —tables R. and L.—mirror over mantel-shelf—pens and ink—books —bell on table—embroidery frame—couch, chairs, etc.*

Enter PAGE, C. *from* L.

PAGE. (*Speaks as he enters.*) I am sorry she is out ! (*Speaking off.*) Tell the brougham to remain—I will wait your mistress's return. (*Gazing about admiringly.*) It is here my Diva reigns—on this couch she reposes—in this mirror her beautiful eyes are reflected ! (*Walking about the room restlessly.*) Let me see what new greeting I can devise—what new compliment pay her. Shall I tell her that she is as beautiful as an angel and simple as a cowslip ? Pshaw ! that don't sound the thing ! angels and cowslips don't go well together !

What a gift it is, to be able to look cruelly charming to the woman you love, and utter some miraculous sentiment that never was thought of before! (*Takes newspaper from pocket, and sits,* L.) Law, bless me! Lord Palmleaf put up again for—um!—(*as if skimming an article*) promises reform, ballot, abolition of—Ah, yes, the old story! promise everything, and do—

Enter MRS. DARLINGTON, C., *followed by* FOOTMAN.

MRS. D. (*Speaking as she enters.*) Remember, Thomas, if the gentleman next door calls, I will hear what he has to say. (*Seeing* PAGE, *who rises.*) Good morning, Mr. Page—I saw your brougham at the door.

PAGE. I have just this moment come. You observe, I make no stranger of myself! (MRS. DARLINGTON *gives bonnet and shawl to* FOOTMAN, *who exits,* R. D.)

MRS. D. I have been over to St. George's to witness a grand wedding. The bride was a beautiful girl, and I should think, not more then nineteen—she looked perfectly radiant in her silken robes! (*Sits,* R.) Poor creature! another victim! Oh, by the way, Mr. Page, I must tell you before I forget it—my new tenant, next door, is very troublesome. He has left his card twice this week, and quite insists on an interview. Isn't it a bore to be harassed in this manner?

PAGE. Perhaps he wishes some repairs.

MRS. D. I have a suspicion that he is an admirer!

PAGE. (*Warmly.*) Eh? you will not receive him then, surely?

MRS. D. (*Laughingly.*) Why should I not? To what am I indebted for such an early visit from you to-day?

PAGE. Most important business, which I'll communicate after—

MRS. D. What?

PAGE. Paying due homage to your beauty.

MRS. D. Now for pity's sake, let me beg of you, as an especial favor, not to do anything of the sort. If you only knew how sick I am of compliments, and you are so lavish of them! Do be more economical in future!

Page. If you were less interesting I might!

Mrs. D. There—there, you must imagine that I am. Be. sides, you remember our compact—you are never to be sentimental in my presence.

Page. But how can a man employ cold words with a flame burning in his breast. (*Sighing.*) An amber flame, if I may so term it, that has burned three long years.

Mrs. D. Don't talk such nonsense, Mr. Page. Three years! I was then under the protection—or, I should rather say, the domination of a husband.

Page. But you have been a widow more than a year.

Mrs. D. And intend remaining one for many more to come.

Page. In other words—I am doomed to love you for ever without hope!

Mrs. D. But what compels you to love me?

Page. Your thousand graces—your wit—your—

Mrs. D. (*Taking a fan from pocket, which she shakes at him.*) You are beginning again!

Page. I stop! (*Placing his hand on his mouth.*)

Mrs. D. I tell you nothing new, when I repeat I have renounced for ever all ideas of matrimony! Heigho! what experience I have had, was—But there is no use of reviving bitter recollections!

Page. You were sacrified!

Mrs. D. Yes, yes—all woman are! My husband, to be sure, had good qualities, but unfortunately, he had possessed them too long! Sixty-two years! and the gout made him irritable, impatient, and fretful—true, he was amiable when in good health, but as he suffered ten months in twelve, you can form an estimate of my happiness!

Page. All you say proves the justice of my position. Now if you had married a superb, dashing fellow—in point of fact, a perfect man—

Mrs. D. (*Banteringly*) Like yourself—

Page. How well you use the privilege of your sex! But e idea of a man of seventy—

Mrs. D. Sixty-two, if you please! Don't make it worse than it was!

Page. Well, sixty-two. Love has lost its bloom, and men marry at that age to be nursed.

Mrs. D. Husbands are much alike, young or old—they are all despotic, treacherous, exacting, or capricious; they are kind and attentive sometimes, I admit, but it's only when the humor takes them. It is honey and caresses one moment, and wormwood and indifference the next. (*Crossing.*) So if you do not wish me to hate you, pray don't love me a minute longer.

Page. Do you think I can dismiss you from my heart as I would a witness from the box. (*Taking paper from his breast pocket.*) You urge me, I find, to the dull business purport of my call this morning. I require your signature to this document, before filing it in the Court of Chancery.

Mrs. D. (*Taking it and signs.*) You lawyers are a world of trouble. It seems that my husband's estate yields nothing but vexation. (*Returning it.*)

Page. Out of which one good arises—I am enabled to see you oftener than I otherwise should.

Mrs. D. Not going to begin again, I hope! I will save your imagination any further trouble by wishing you good morning, Mr. Page. (*Aside.*) Provoking creature! if he would only worship me less, I believe I should love him ten times better.   [*Exit*, R.

Page. (*Pacing the stage.*) Well, she is either the most indifferent woman in the world, or has a happy knack of seeming so. Her heart is as impregnable as a fortress. She has the most implicit confidence in me in all affairs save those of love. If I were a fool, or even ugly or deformed, I could in some measure account for her coldness, but—(*Pausing opposite mirror and regarding himself.*) Confound the thing—a countenance like mine ought to do something for me.

Enter Sir Charles Ripple, D.—*he strolls in leisurely, and speaks off as he enters.*

Sir C. Yes, yes, it is quite right—I'll wait till your mistress returns.

PAGE. (*Seeing him—aside.*) Who is that?

SIR C. A man here—not favorable!

PAGE. (*Aside.*) What a striking likeness to Sir Charles Ripple!

SIR C. (*Aside.*) He's confoundedly like Lyttleton Page.

PAGE (*Bowing.*) 1 beg your pardon! (*Aside.*) It must be.

SIR C. (*After a mutual glance of recognition.*) I am sure of it. (*Aloud.*) Why, Page, how are you? (*Extending his hand.*)

PAGE. Sir Charles! I thought it was you the moment I set eyes on you. I'm glad to see you. It has been two years since we met!

SIR C. Quite right! I've been home from Italy these three months. And how goes the world with you, Page—the London world—still a bachelor?

PAGE. Still a bachelor; but fiercely in love, notwithstanding.

SIR C. A lawyer in love! ha, ha! Cupid and Coke! what a partnership!

PAGE. It's folly to suppose a man is master of his own heart!

SIR C. The popular notion is that your profession is not troubled with that organ.

PAGE. In my case, popular idea is in error, for in the matter of heart, the deficit is on the side of the lady!

SIR C. Do you mean to say she has rejected you?

PAGE. I fear so; and the unfortunate part of the business is, leaving my bruised feelings out of the case, she is worth five thousand pounds a-year!

SIR C. Now I clearly understand your emotion—I can sympathise with you!

PAGE. It has not been for want of enterprise, I assure you—I have been most attentive—slavishly so; and as for compliments, I have positively ransacked my library for graceful images and glowing fancies to embroider my conversation.

SIR C. And do you suppose your "ladye fair" doesn't understand embroidery better than yourself?

PAGE. I believe she would reject the advances of any man, though he were as tender as Romeo, impassioned as Petrarch, persuasive as Mephistopheles, and elegant as Chesterfield. Mrs. Darlington, I fear, is unconquerable.

SIR C. Oh, is she the object of your affections?

PAGE. Do you know her? of course you do!

SIS C. No, I do not *yet!*

PAGE. (*With surprise.*) Then how is it I find you in this drawing-room?

SIR C. This is the first time I was ever here in my life! everything must have a beginning, even an acquaintance with a lady!

PAGE. But if you do not know her, by what right or what plea are you here! I confess I was never so amazed in my life!

SIR P. Then if you *must* know, I rented of her agent the house next door a few weeks since, and this is a visit of respect. True, it is not exactly an English custom—our civilization is so deplorably humdrum. I picked it up in Venice —*haute galanterie,* you perceive ; and a tenant, if he be well bred and well travelled should—

PAGE. Come, come, Sir Charles, don't shelter your motives under the house next door.

SIR C. Don't be jealous, my dear Page. Although neighbors, we have never exchanged kisses at the window, nor forget-me-nots by moonlight!

PAGE. Still fond of adventure, Sir Charles?

SIR C. As Childe Harold or a troubadour, and would go as far in quest of it.

PAGE. (*With perplexity.*) Yes, yes, oh yes! (*Aside.*) I trust he will not display his love of adventure under this roof.

SIR P. (*Aside.*) Jealous already, and perplexed as well!

PAGE. Your object, I perceive, is to make love to Mrs. Darlington, and I frankly tell you that you might as well save yourself the trouble.

SIR C. (*Interruptingly.*) Trouble! ha, ha!

PAGE. You have the example of my failure before you eyes.

SIR C. You are one man. Venus married Vulcan, a filthy blacksmith, after having refused a dozen excellent offers, at least. It requires no ballooning in metaphysics, to demonstrate the caprice and wilfulness of women.

PAGE. (*Gravely.*) But I assure you she dislikes *all* men. She avers they are despotic, capricious, exacting, and cruel. What delights other women enrages her; and as to her opinions, they are always opposite to your own. Now what can one do to shift hers round to yours?

SIR C. Always be of hers, and there will be no occasion for her to change. It is a vast mistake to differ with a woman on any point. I have a theory of my own that a woman can be won by indifference sooner than any other method.

PAGE. It don't strike me.

SIR C. How long have you known Mrs. Darlington?

PAGE. Let me see—three—nearly four years.

SIR C. The enigma is solved—you have known her too long, If I undertook to lay siege to a heart, I would answer to carrying it at three assaults. Come, Page, I will deal frankly with you. I confess I was captivated by your charming widow; and it was perfectly natural for me, as a next door neighbor, to cultivate her acquaintance, if possible! But much as I admire her, I resign my intentions, unless—Now it occurs to me that I can serve you and illustrate my doctrine, that women are soonest won by indifference. What do you say—shall we become affiliated like the *Illuminati,* and engage in the cause with one heart? It will cost me a pang, but that is nothing where the happiness of a friend is involved. What do you say—shall we unite our forces and strengthen our means of attack? The affair will amuse me; and it's a sad case if two man can't win the heart of one woman.

PAGE. Sir Charles, you are distinguished for your ingenuity and power of reasoning. You might succeed in inducing her to believe me worthy of her serious consideration. This rencontre is most fortunate! Perhaps if I had not met you.

the widow would have been lost to me for ever. And what a loss it would have been—such a delightful woman!

SIR C. And five thousand a-year—you shouldn't forget that!

PAGE. Now, I shall leave the affair in your hands. (*Aside.*) Courting by deputy may not be *en régle*, but as I can do nothing unaided in the case, I cannot help but benefit by junior counsel. (*Aloud.*) *Au revoir!* I shall soon be with you again. [*Exit*, C.

SIR C. I always knew Lyttleton Page to be a somewhat feeble individual, but if any one had told me that he was such a consummate blockhead, I would have kicked the informer. The idea, in this nineteenth century, of creature No. 1 trusting fellow creature No. 2 to erect a temple of love for creature No. 1 to inhabit, and the temple worth five thousand pounds a-year, passes belief.

Enter MRS DARLINGTON, R., *speaking as she enters.*

MRS. D. Some one here, and unannounced! (*To* RIPPLES.) I beg pardon, sir—whom have I the pleasure of addressing? (*He rises, bows, and hands her his card.*) This is not the first card of yours that has been put into my hands. I think "not at home" was always the reply, which, to a man of discernment, is sufficiently obvious!

SIR C. I must crave your pardon, for one moment. I have the honor of being your tenant. and at the same moment your very humble servant. I have been residing abroad for some years, and it is the custom in Venice for all tenants to pay a visit of respect to their *proprietaire*, especially if it be a lady!

MRS. D. But you are now in England—London and Venice are widely different.

SIR C. Truly, but I also wish to consult you—

MRS. D. (*Interruptingly.*) About some repairs, I presume?

SIR G. (*Catching at the idea.*) Yes, yes, precisely! (*Aside.*) She assists me. (*Aloud.*) One of the chimneys smokes like Vesuvius before an eruption.

Mrs. D. My man of business shall send you a bricklayer! It was scarcely necessary to wait on me to tell me a chimney smoked! Perhaps that, too, is a Venetian custom!

Sir C. You have anticipated my assurance on that point. (*Pointing to the couch.*) I beg pardon, would you have the kindness to be seated?

Mrs. D. Sir!

Sir C. It grieves me to see you stand.

Mrs. D. But, sir, it seems to me that it is I who—(*Aside.*) Was there ever such cool audacity. He is positively doing the honor of my own house.

Sir C. Let me beg of you—

Mrs. D. Since you insist on it, thank you! (*Sits at table, R.*) His *sang froid* is positively amusing.

Sir C. You are extremely gracious to respect my desire! (*Aside.*) I am getting on!

Mrs. D. It's clear he must not be encouraged! (*Takes embroidery frame, turns her back, and begins working.*)

Sir C. (*Aside.*) I don't wonder Page adores her—she *is* a charming woman! (*Turns over leaves of books on table—a slight silence.*)

Mrs. D. Although presumptuous, he has not much to say for himself! (*Looking round.*) I declare, he is reading!

Sir C. (*Reads.*) "Oh, thou in Hellas deemed of heavenly birth!"

Mrs. D. I beg your pardon, did you speak?

Sir C. Not at all.

Mrs. D. I regret interrupting you!

Sir C. Pray don't mention it! (*He continues reading, and she embroiders.*)

Mrs. D. (*Aside.*) What a bear he is! (*Aloud.*) Hem!

Sir C. Hem!

Mrs. D. Hem! (*Aside.*) If these are Venetian manners, I prefer our plain English customs! (*Aloud.*) Are you aware, Sir Charles Ripple, that in England a visit involves something more than reading?

Sir C. (*Closing the book.*) True—I was absorbed!

MRS. D. And you a traveller, too! one would imagine you glowing with reminiscence! The Forum by moonlight, a sunrise from Monte Rosa, a morning at Versailles, an excursion on Lake Leman, a drive on the Bois de Boulogne, or a promenade in Naples, might surely suggest a conversation. The enchantment of Venice, where you have resided, should make eloquent any man with soul.

SIR C. Granted—if they had not been described to death. Everybody who could put pen to paper, or pencil to canvas for the last three centuries, has had a fling at Venice. I may, therefore, hold myself exempt from so hackneyed a theme, and shall not inflict on you so much as the description of a gondola.

MRS. D. (*Aside.*) Convenient sophistry!

SIR C. (*After a brief pause.*) I think we shall have rain before night.

She makes no reply—he hums a melody, and again resumes his reading.

MRS. D. Are you musical?

SIR C. I play a little on the drum!

MRS. D. A brilliant accomplishment! (*Ironically.*) And Venetian, I presume. I fear you dislike conversation?

SIR C. Not I—but casual visiting is so fatal to unreserved utterance. We might chat for an hour and get no further than common places! It would seem inappropriate, if not eccentric, for me to say anything eloquent or sincere!

MRS. D. It is a woman's prerogative to gossip! Besides, it is so easy, and requires no mental strain! One can't be always on stilts!

SIR C. Do you know that in Venice conversation is quite gone out of fashion? The practice has degenerated to lawyers, and men of that stamp.

MRS. D. It is odd you should make that remark, for I was about to observe that a legal friend of mine, Mr. Lyttleton Page, never opens his lips in my presence but out falls a vow, or a compliment.

SIR C. I am surprised that any lady of sense will listen

to vows which I liken to I, O, U's, with which the bankrupt of one sex pays to the other the debts of its heart.

MRS. D. Your simile is that of a commercial traveller, who has been jilted!

SIR C. One feels a degree of latitude in speaking of an intimate friend!

MRS. D. (*Aside.*) An intimate friend! (*Aloud.*) I was not aware that you knew Mr. Page! He is one of the most gallant men alive—his compliments are masterpieces.

SIR C. (*Aside.*) Filched from his library by his own confession. (*Shaking his head.*) Humph!

MRS. D. (*Ironically.*) You are extremely civil, I must confess! I don't see the harm of a few courtiers!

SIR C. They went out with coaching, high heels, patches, and powder. They were all very well as toadies to the Charleses, and it answered the purpose of Louis Quatorze to cultivate the breed—but depend upon it they have lost their power.

MRS. D. Ours is imperishable!

SIR C. While your beauty remains—where such a thing exists!

MRS. D. (*Aside.*) Can that remark have a personal tendency? (*Aloud.*) I fear I have the misfortune, then, in your eyes, not to be agreeable?

SIR C. I have aroused her vanity, that's something. (*Aloud.*) Oh, you are still well enough!

MRS. D. Still? For gracious sake, do I look like a grandmother?

SIR C. Heaven forbid!

MRS. D. Your insinuation was most unpleasant! and allow me to add, if I do look old, it is premature, produced by two years of married life, sadness, and suffering.

SIR C. Your husband must have been very unhappy.

MRS. D. May I inquire why?

SIR C. It is the usual lot of husbands, and I cannot suppose that yours escaped more favored then the rest. (*Aside.*) That ought to excite her!

MRS. D. (*Glancing at the card.*) Permit me to say, Sir Charles Ripple, that it is my sex who are the real sufferers.

SIR C. A mistake, madam. A bitter experience has taught me the truth of what I urge. I am a widower.

MRS. D. Perhaps you were unfortunate in your choice?

SIR C. To tell you the truth, I believe wives are all, more or less alike, coquettish, fidgety, vain, and frivolous! My wife was a glorious woman when in good health, but unfortunately she was an invalid twelve months in the year!

MRS. D. (*Aside.*) How his experience rhymes with my own! (*A'oud.*) I maintain, all women are not what you assert—and I further assert that there are faultless women!

SIR C. They must inhabit the moon, then—I have discovered none on this planet!

MRS. D. I perceive you do not veil your opinions.

SIR C. To be sincere, requires heroism—and few are courageous enough to express their convictions.

MRS. D. Whether those convictions be acceptable or otherwise to those with whom you seek contact.

SIR C. I fear I have offended you, and lest my candor cause you pain, I will retire. (*Taking his hat.*) I have the honor of wishing you good morning. (*Going up*, C.)

MRS. D. Good morning, Sir Charles Ripple. (*Aside.*) Confound the man! his very rudeness has something in it that interests me!

SIR C. (*Returning a few steps.*) When shall I have the honor of seeing Mrs. Darlington again?

MRS. D. There is no hurry!

SIR C. (*Aside.*) Which liberally construed, means, as soon as I please. (*Aloud.*) Depend upon it I shall pay you another visit, if that chimney continues smoking! (*Bowing.*) Good morning, madam! [*Exit*, C.

MRS. D. I never, until this moment, suspected myself of possessing too much amiability; but it occurs to me I was off my guard with that provoking man! To allow a stranger to tell me that women are all coquettish, vain, frivolous!

it is too much: *Takes up book, turns over the leaves, and throws it down on table, impatiently.*)

Enter PAGE, *door* C.

Oh, Mr. Page, I am glad you have returned!

PAGE. (*Aside.*) Already glad! how well he has pleaded my cause!

MRS. D. I am very angry—very angry, indeed!

PAGE. Temper does not affect your voice, then—it is the soul of music!

MRS. D. (*Aside.*) After what I have just experienced, a compliment is not unacceptable.

PAGE. A rather curious circumstance causes me to return so soon! I must tell you frankly that I did not know the adversary in one of your suits—having left the preliminaries to my managing clerk, and on looking over the papers, I discover, to my surprise, that it is Sir Charles Ripple, one of my most valued friends.

MRS. D. Who has but this moment quitted the room—

PAGE. Can it be possible? He's a most agreeable fellow, is he not? Brave and noble, and the very pink of gallantry! (*Aside.*) I must place my colleague in as good a light as possible. (*Aloud.*) Did he speak of me?

MRS. D. (*Smiling.*) In the most extraordinary terms!

PAGE. (*Aside.*) Generous creature! (*Aloud.*) Poor Sir Charles! in some respects he has been very unfortunate!

MRS. D. I suppose you mean in regard to his wife?

PAGE. I never knew he was married!

MRS. D. (*Aside.*) Was he deceiving me?

PAGE. In consideration of his misfortunes, I have come to propose—

MRS. D. (*Apart, abstractedly.*) But what was his motive for doing so?

PAGE. (*Endeavoring to engage her attention.*) To propose—

MRS. D. (*Still apart, pacing the room.*) Did he descend to a falsehood, that he might the more effectually rail against women?

PAGE. (*Following her.*) To propose an amicable settlement. (*Aside.*) What's the matter with her, I wonder?

MRS. D. (*Aside.*) And I was weak enough to listen to his cruel reproaches! If he dare call here again, I'll prove to him that I am able to defend my much injured sex. (*Sits at table.*)

PAGE. I repeat, Mrs. Darlington, that in order to avoid delay, to say nothing of exposure. it will be better to adjust this affair by arbitration

Enter SIR CHARLES.

Here he is!

SIR C. (*Bowing.*) A thousand pardons, madam!

PAGE. Well met, Sir Charles—your name was on my tongue as you entered the door. I was suggesting—

SIR C. (*Apart, in an undertone.*) Find an excuse to leave us at once!

PAGE. (*Apart.*) I comprehend you—we are getting on famously!

SIR C. (*Apart.*) No delay—every moment is of value.

PAGE. (*Apart.*) Exercise all your eloquence!

MRS. D (*Apart.*) What is all that buzzing about?

PAGE. My dear Mrs. Darlington, an engagement near at hand demands my presence for a few moments. (*To her.*) You will pardon this abruptness. (*To* SIR CHARLES.) Day day, Sir Charles! (*Aside.*) How fortunate am I to have at my elbow so able an advocate in the court of Cupid.

[*Exit,* c.

SIR C. (*Aside.*) The widow is glancing poignards this way. I must soothe her.

MRS. D. Sir Charles Ripple, you seem to run in and out of my house, as if it were the Exchange or a hotel. You forget, sir, what is due to a lady.

SIR C. Don't charge me with so deplorable an offence. I confess this visit would seem abrupt, had I not returned for my gloves.

MRS. D. (*Turning her eyes about the room, and then observing his hands.*) Unless suffering some optical delusion, it strikes me that your gloves are precisely where they should be—on your hands.

SIR C. (*Affecting surprise.*) Why so they are. I begin to suspect myself of bewilderment of intellect, absence of mind, or some disastrous affliction. I was as profoundly convinced of the idea that I left my gloves here as I am that St. Paul's has a dome. (*Removing one of his gloves deliberately.*)

MRS. D. (*Aside.*) Does he take me for an imbecile to believe such nonsense? He evidently admires me, and that is the secret! (*Aloud.*) I must say your remissness is, indeed, strange; and allow me to add that your calls are too rapid to be agreeable.

SIR C. (*Retiring.*) I fear I inconvenience you?

MRS. D. Trifles never put me out of the way.

SIR C. Hem! (*Aside.*) Then I may dare to regard this as another call! (*Sits.*) You are—

MRS. D. (*Quickly.*) Coquettish, vain, and frivolous, like the rest of my sex, I suppose.

SIR C. (*Aside.*) Piqued and interested—'tis well!

MRS. D. *Apropos,* I have just been talking with your friend, Mr. Page—

SIR C. It must have afforded you great pleasure.

MRS. D. You were the subject of our conversation.

SIR C. Then I am sure you were delighted!

MRS. D. (*Aside.*) Vain coxcomb! (*Aloud.*) I said I was speaking of you—I should rather have said of your wife Mr. Page could give me no information concerning her.

SIR C. (*Aside.*) Invention assist me! (*Speaking slowly, and seeming to invent as he proceeds.*) Oh yes, that is easily explained—he never saw her. I married in Corsica, and my bride never came to England. My marriage was a curious whim, I confess. She was the daughter of a brigand—a pale, delicate, spiritual-looking creature. It was a strange, romantic, unhappy affair. It would pain you to hear the details. (*Aside.*) For a fib at short notice, that must answer

Mrs. D. You tell me sufficient to understand your opinions of women. You find yourself in Corsica, that hot-bed of vile passions, and by your own confession wed the offspring of a robber, whom you set up as a standard by whom to judge ladies generally. It is a noble mission to bring you—when I say *you*, I mean any man, to his senses.

Sir C. What means will you employ?

Mrs. D. By remarrying myself, and proving that I am a faultless woman.

Sir C. You are, indeed, heroic!

Mrs. D. I'll make an especial point of adoring my husband! coquetry shall never enter my head—I'll take care that vanity and I are not on visiting terms—frivolity shall be set aside for a calm sense of duty. In short, sir, I'll make my husband a happy man, pierced by no regrets that he did not visit the moon in search of a wife.

Sir C. What charming vengeance! Now, may I inquire who is to be the happy man, for I presume you have made your choice?

Mrs. D. I can't see that it concerns you—

Sir C. Nay, though, had I a list of your acquaintance, I should be tempted to guess.

Mrs. D. You seem to be interested!

Sir C. (*Warmly.*) I am, very much! (*Recovering himself.*) As much, madam, as a stranger dare be under the circumstances.

Mrs. D. (*Aside.*) He improves on acquaintance. (*Aloud.*) It's no very great secret, after all. I don't know why I should not tell you. It is—

Enter a Footman, *announcing.*

Footman. Mr Lyttleton Page!

Enter Page, *with umbrella.*

Page. Soon returned, you see! good gracious, how it is raining! It is only a passing shower, though!

Mrs. D. (*To* Sir Charles.) My servant, you see, spared me the confusion of mentioning the name. (*To* Page.) Mr.

Page, don't wet the carpet, if you please! Leave your umbrella in the hall.

PAGE. How stupid of me! I really beg your pardon! (*Aside to* SIR CHARLES.) I hope I have not returned too quickly.   [*Exit* C., *with umbrella.*

SIR C. I congratulate you on your choice.

MRS. D You are very kind!

SIR C. I think him the man, of all others, suited to you.

MRS. D. (*Emphatically.*) Precisely my opinion!

PAGE *re-enters, or as she says this.*

PAGE. May I ask what is your opinion?

MRS. D. (*Looking at watch—rises.*) That I have a few orders to give my servant, and must leave you a moment, my dear Mr. Page, with Sir Charles Ripple!

PAGE. (*Aside.*) She said my dear Mr Page!

SIR C. (*Rising.*) I hope I shall have the pleasure of seeing Mrs. Darlington again?

MRS. D. (*Carelessly.*) If you are passing at some distant period, I shall be very glad!

SIR C. (*Bowing.*) Your condescension is profound! (*He offers his arm to conduct her to the door—*PAGE *does the same—she accepts his and exits,* R.

MRS. D. (*To* PAGE.) Au revoir!

SIR C. (*Aside.*) Page will be ready to jump out of his skin!

PAGE. (*Seizing* SIR CHARLES *by the hands.*) My dear Sir Charles, you have performed miracles!

SIR C. (*Aside.*) He must not win her easily—I must torture him a little!

PAGE. I am confident my suit is progressing.

SIR C. After the fashion of a crab—backwards.

PAGE. Eh? what do you mean?

SIR C. All my eloquence is lost on her.

PAGE. But I observe a change in her manner. She called me "dear Mr. Page" just now, a thing she rarely does, expect in a blooming temper.

SIR C. I am aware of all that, but lawyer as you are, you do not seem to detect the weak points of your client's case. Those soft words are the mere delusive prologue to something extremely disagreeable that is to follow. So don't be off your guard.

PAGE. Can it be possible?

SIR C. Stay a moment. You shall be spared the pain and mortification of the scheme she meditates—anticipate her cruelty by assuring her in distinct terms that your affection was only feigned.

PAGE. She would be furious!

SIR C. There you go! women are beyond the pale of your comprehension. Do you suppose their exquisite perception is blinded by idle compliments, which, after all, are mere prismatic bubbles blown with the softest of soap. Believe, me, indifference is the only true plan. At first they will detest you, but in the end they will determine to reform you by making you adore them. Be advised—change your system.

PAGE. By Jove, I believe you are right. I have tried honey for a long time to no purpose.

SIR C. Sweets clog! the reign of sapphires and fairies is over. You may flatter like the book of beauty, but it will not serve your purpose.

PAGE. For an experiment, I *will* change my system. I'll assure Mrs. Darlington that the wedding-ring should be of iron—not gold.

SIR C. Quite right!

PAGE. That women are all vain!

SIR C. Capital!

PAGE. And coquettish!

SIR C. Bravo!

PAGE. And that in courting her society I was only in search of a sensation.

SIR C. You'll take her by storm. Her surprise will be something marvellous. I'll leave you together at once, and strike while the determination is warm upon you. Show

her that your accustomed honey has fermented, and that
your complimentary sugar has fallen in the market. (*Aside.*)
What fun, to lead them into a cloud. (*Aloud.*) I wish you
all the success this change of system deserves.   [*Exit*, C.

PAGE. I fear I shall proceed awkwardly, though. It will
seem clumsy to mix up compliments and cruelty—a pane-
gyric in one breath and a reproach the next. (*Drawing himself up.*) But I'll be as brutal as common decency will permit. If there is anything in this cold water system, I'll
spare no pains in ascertaining it.

Enter MRS. DARLINGTON, R.

MRS. D. My dear Mr. Page, I hope you will not think
me rude in quitting you just now?

PAGE. (*Aside.*) "My dear Mr. Page!" How artful women are! I am not to be trapped so easily, she will find!
(*Aloud.*) Tra, la, la!

MRS. D. A serious mischance with my milliner must be
my excuse! (*Looking at him.*) Why, what under the sun is
the matter with the man? Ha, ha!

PAGE. (*Aside.*) She is laughing at me! She sees that I
am acting! I shall never be able to keep it up! (*Aloud.*)
Eh? what's the matter with me? Hem! I am thinking—
thinking.

MRS. D. Can't you think without putting your nose in
the air in that manner?

PAGE. Yes—yes—madam!

MRS. D. Why say madam?—it sounds harshly between
friends!

PAGE. (*Aside.*) Between friends! How well she does it!

MRS. D. You and I have known each other for a long
time!

PAGE. True—and in that time what a deal of idle twaddle
I have uttered. I almost blush to think of it

MRS. D. You have told me that I was bewitching, and
lovely, and enchanting, and—I forget what else!

PAGE. Ay, I remember—I seem as if awaking from a
chronic stupor.

Mrs. D. Then do you mean to say that I am not bewitching?

Page. (*Warmly.*) To be sure you—(*Arresting himself.*) I am no judge of beauty! (*Aside.*) I am sure I shall spoil it.

Mrs. D. Mr. Page, do you know what you are saying?

Page. Perfectly.

Mrs. D. And that I am not lovely?

Page. Many may think you so.

Mrs. D. Nor enchanting?

Page. Now, seriously, did you believe all the badinage I uttered to amuse myself? Oh, women are, indeed, vain!

Mrs. D. Mr. Lyttleton Page—sir! you are my legal adviser, it is true, but in this case, I must take the law in my own hands!

Page. Believe me, it could not be in bet—(*Aside.*) Hallo! what am I about?—just going to pay her another compliment.

Mrs. D. I say, sir, I must take the law into my own hands, and you will be kind enough to remember to whom you are speaking!

Page. My memory scarcely needs refreshing.

Mrs. D. I ask, sir, what is the meaning of this conduct? Half an hour ago, were I Juno, you could not have paid me more homage.

Page. (*Aside.*) She's touched! Sir Charles is right! A change of system *was* required. (*Aloud.*) The fact is, I have been seriously thinking of what you so earnestly assured me. Did you not say that if I did not wish you to hate me I must cease loving you?

Mrs. D. It is true, I did say so—but I have been thinking as well as yourself.

Page. (*Aside.*) I am not to be caught by such speeches. My colleague has taught me a trick worth two of that. (*Aloud.*) Have you not on all occasions assured me that my compliments were oppressive rather than pleasing, and that you had renounced for ever all ideas of matrimony?

Mrs. D. You do not seem to understand women!

PAGE. (*Aside.*) Just what Sir Charles says!

MRS. D. They often say things they don't mean!

PAGE. (*Aside.*) They do, indeed!

MRS. D. Heigho! This goes to show me how little, after all, we know of each other! Suppose I had said to myself, "Mr. Page is an agreeable person, not handsome, to be sure, but still well-looking enough—and—"

PAGE. (*Aside.*) It will not do!

MRS. D. "And in consideration of his long and ardent devotion, although I do not particularly love him, I will bestow upon him my hand."

PAGE. (*Quickly.*) What, have you, then, accepted my numerous proposals? (*Aside.*) What am I about?

MRS. D. (*With emphasis.*) I am putting a case—I said *suppose!*

PAGE. (*Aside.*) That is the crevice by which she escapes! (*Aloud.*) Then *I* should say, "Your condescension is very magnanimous—but as marriage is a very serious matter, I desire time for reflection."

MRS. D. Then suppose I demanded an immediate answer?

PAGE. I should insist upon a brief period for consideration!

MRS. D. And if it did not please me to grant it?

PAGE. Why, then, the only chance left for me in that case, would be to distinctly—(*with an effort*) refuse!

MRS. D. So, so! very good! (*Ringing the bell.*)

PAGE. (*Aside—proudly.*) It cost me a pang—but I said it!

Enter FOOTMAN.

MRS. D Mr. Page wishes an escort to the door! (*Aside.*) My feelings shall not be trifled with in this manner. (*Walks stage.*)

PAGE. (*Aside.*) The door! I have exceeded proper limits, and—(*Aloud—confused.*) Pardon me, Mrs. Darlington, when I said that—it was with no intention, I assure you, of—it was only my desire to—(*Aside.*) I am making a nice mess of it!

MRS. D. (*To* FOOTMAN.) You have heard my orders! (*The* FOOTMAN *gives him his hat.*)

PAGE. (*Taking it, and bowing.*) Oh, don't for an instant fancy that your word is not law! (*Aside.*) This change of system has succeeded with a vengeance! but I'll return for an explanation when she has calmed down a little! (*Aloud.*) Adieu, madam, adieu!   [*Exit,* C., *followed by* FOOTMAN.

MRS. D. (*Walking about the room in an excited manner.*) It is impossible for a man to exchange affection for indifference, and devotion for coldness, in this rapid manner. I am convinced that there is—I see it all—it is the work of this Mephistopheles—this Sir Charles Ripple—he is schooling Page into his own wicked estimate of women! What a triumph it would be to bring the master to my feet, and make him acknowledge a defeat! (*Reflecting for a moment.*) I will! (*Resuming her embroidery.*)

Enter SIR CHARLES, C., *hastily—he has his hat on.*

SIR C. Once more I must throw myself on your indul-gence. (*Looking about the room.*)

MRS. D. Well, sir, what is the matter now?

SIR C. Pray do not disturb yourself! Where could I have put it?

MRS. D. (*Aside.*) What can he wish?

SIR C. (*Ambling about the room.*) It's very strange! I cannot see it!

MRS. D (*Rising.*) What do you wish? Perhaps I can assist you?

SIR C. I am looking for my hat—I am sure I left it here!

MRS. D. It is on your head.

SIR C. (*Removing it.*) I must be out of my senses! Instead of my hat it is my brain I have lost—perhaps my heart, who knows? (*Bowing.*) I have the honor—good morning! (*As if retiring.*)

MRS. D. As you seem to do nothing but run up and down stairs, I think you had better remain where you are. This is your third call this morning.

SIR C. So it is. You are the soul of kindness! (*Puts down hat, and sits.*)

MRS. D. Do you know there is an awful epidemic going about?

SIR C. The cholera?

MRS. D. No—impertinence; and your friend, Mr. Page, has got it to perfection.

SIR C. Is it possible? Where could he have contracted it I wonder?

MRS. D. (*Ironically.*) I cannot imagine. Would you believe it, he is positively so infected that he has had the audacity to refuse my hand.

SIR C. His case must be a desperate one.

MRS. D. Is it not dreadful to think of? The man I had settled on in my own mind—in fact, the only man I know in the wide would who would have borne with my imperfections! and he to desert me at the very moment I had determined to vindicate the reputation of my sex!

SIR C. Shameful to the last degree! (*Sighing.*) I would I were he.

MRS. D. What do you say?

SIR C. That I might assist you in this glorious vindication. A noble resolve should never be overthrown for want of encouragement.

MRS. D. (*Aside.*) So—so, my friend!

SIR C. It is so seldom that a lady possessing grace, beauty, and intelligence will take the pains to demonstrate a great truth.

MRS. D. (*Aside.*) He retracts. (*Aloud.*) From that remark, I judge you do not esteem my sex so lightly.

SIR C. (*With sangfroid.*) No, no—there are special cases —grand exceptions to all general rules.

MRS. D. But where are you to find this grace, beauty, and intelligence of which you speak?

SIR C. (*Pointing to* MRS. DARLINGTON.) There.

MRS. D. (*Looking around her.*) There! where?

SIR C. Clustered in you.

Mrs. D. Ha, ha! What, do you think me beautiful?

Sir C. That has been my opinion from the very first moment I beheld you.

Mrs. D. Are you really serious?

Sir C. I was never half so earnest in my life!

Mrs. D. You are positively growing gallant, absolutely paying me compliments! You, too, of all others, who never flatter any one! Why, what has become of all your ice?

Sir C. Melted in the sunshine of your presence.

Mrs. D. And in so short a time?

Sir C. Its rays were powerful. Perhaps I am recovering from the epidemic that is going about.

Mrs. D. Then you confess to being touched?

Sir C. Slightly. But I think you have wrought a cure!

Mrs D. I must have proofs to convince me!

Sir C. How can I offer them?

Mrs. D. By professing a firm faith, acknowledging your faults, and an open avowal of the universal perfection of woman.

Sir C. Of—all?

Mrs. D. A penitent should never hesitate!

Sir C. I confess that I am embarrassed.

Mrs. D. (*Aside.*) All the better! (*Aloud.*) Step the first— get on your knees.

Sir C. On my knees! (*Aside.*) The attitude is anything but pleasant. (*Kneeling on one knee.*) Behold me at your feet!

Mrs. D. You are on one knee—that will never do—your sins require two.

Sir C. There! (*Kneels.*)

Mrs. D. (*Aside.*) I have triumphed—glorious! (*Aloud.*) Now repeat, "I abjure my heresy—I acknowledge my errors."

Sir C. (*With mock humility.*) "I abjure my heresy and acknowledge my errors." (*Aside.*) How ridiculous this is.

Mrs. D. "I ask pardon of all the ladies for sins I have charged them with." (*He repeats it.*) "And I promise for the future to respect and honor them."

Sir C. (*Warmly—aside.*) Now for it! (*Aloud.*) As a body, collectively speaking, but to love only one—yourself—whom I will cherish till time everlasting.

Mrs. D. What do I hear?

Sir C. That I am a culprit, converted by you whose pardon I implore! (*Seizing her hand and kissing it.*)

Mrs. D. Sir Charles Ripple, what are you about?

Sir C. Doing penance for my sins—my manifold sins. (*Kissing her hand again.*)

Enter Page, c.

Page. (*Speaking as he enters.*) I must not let another moment pass without a thorough explanation. (*Perceiving* Sir Charles *on his knees.*) What do I see—eh? fire and fury!

Sir C. (*Aside.*) Now for warm work! (*Rising.*) My dear Page, you arrive most opportunely. I know you delight in seeing your fellow man happy. Behold me the picture of bliss!

Page. Don't talk to me of bliss, sir—your happiness be—

Sir C. Ah ha! choose your words.

Page. Be hanged! I hasten to explain to my dear Mrs. Darlington my stupidity.

Mrs. D. (*Aside.*) I suspect it—Page is the victim of an intrigue!

Page. I wish to explain, my dear Mrs. Darlington, that my refusal was all on my part a mere stratagem—a change of system—a—

Sir C. (*Coughing to silence him, and laughing aside.*) Hem! hem! hem!

Mrs. D. Stratagem—change of system—what does he mean, Sir Charles?

Sir C. Why do you ask me?

Page. (*Aside.*) He is playing me false! (*Aloud.*) Do you mean to say, Sir Charles Ripple, that you did not advise me to change my system?

Sir C. (*To* Mrs Darlington.) Do you know that I think our mutual and valued friend is touched here! (*Placing finger on forehead with mock gravity.*)

PAGE. (*Pacing the room frantically*) I am a dupe—an idiot —fool that I was to entrust my heart to the diplomacy of a man of the world like Sir Charles Ripple. (*Goes up stage.*)

SIR C. (*Aside.*) Poor Page! he is enduring the agony of the Spartan with the gnawing fox hid under his cloak, and the charming widow—I do believe there is a tear in her eye.

MRS. D. (*Turning aside with emotion.*) I was wrong to listen to him for one moment.

PAGE. (*Coming down furiously.*) Sir Charles Ripple, I pronounced you a traitor, and I demand—

SIR C. Instant satisfaction, which you shall have without resorting to either foils or pistols, which happily belong to a past age—at least, in England. Mrs. Darlington, I scarcely know how to sufficiently apologize for obtruding myself in an affair which at all times concerns but two hearts. The truth is, I found my friend Page writhing under the conviction that his love was unrequited. Ten minutes in your society proved the contrary In a gay moment I proposed an alliance—nay, do not smile—he accepted, and we have enacted a little comedy—farce—what shall I call it?

MRS. D. And the hero is—

SIR C. Mr. Lyttleton Page, who retained me without fee or reward to take his heart out of Chancery. (*With a glance at* MRS. DARLINGTON.) And I think I have succeeded.

PAGE. Forgive my suspicions; but it was exasperating, you must own, to find you on your knees.

SIR C. And now, madam, I throw up my brief—the case is won, and I claim your pardon. And after all, Page, though my theories at first sight may want in a certain consistency, you must acknowledge *your* suit has prospered not a little by a CHANGE OF SYSTEM.

CURTAIN.

THE CITIZEN AND THE THIEVES.

ANONYMOUS.

A CITIZEN, for recreation's sake,
To see the country would a journey take
Some dozen miles, or very little more ;
Taking his leave with friends two months before,
With drinking healths and shaking by the hand,
As he had travelled to some new-found land.
Well, taking horse, with very much ado,
London he leaveth for a day or two :
And as he rideth, meets upon the way
Such as (what haste soever) bid men stay.
" Sirrah ! " says one, " stand and your purse deliver,
I am a *taker*, thou must be a *giver*."

Unto a wood hard by, they haul him in,
And rifle him unto his very skin.
"Masters," quoth he, " pray hear me ere you go ;
For you have robbed me more than you do know,
My horse, in truth, I borrow'd of my brother ;
The bridle and the saddle of another ;
The jerkin and the bases be a tailor's ;
The scarf, I do assure, is a sailor's ;
The falling band is likewise none of mine,
Nor cuffs, as true as this good light doth shine.
The satin doublet, and raised velvet hose,
Are our churchwarden's, all the parish knows.
The boots are John the grocer's at the Swan ;
The spurs were lent me by a serving man.
One of my rings—that with the great red stone—
In sooth, I borrow'd of my neighbor Joan ;
Her husband knows not of it.   Gentlemen !
Thus stands my case—I pray show favor then."

" Why," quoth the thieves, " thou needst not greatly care,
Since in thy loss so many bear a share ;
The world goes hard, and many good folks lack.

Look not, at this time, for a penny back.
Go, tell in London, thou didst meet with four,
That, rifling thee, have robbed at least a score."

BOGGS'S DOGS.

ANONYMOUS.

Did you ever hear of Jehosaphat Boggs,
A dealer and raiser of all sorts of dogs?
"No?" Then I'll endeavor in doggerel verse
To just the main points of the story rehearse.
Boggs had a good wife, the joy of his life,
There was nothing between them inclining to strife,
Except her dear J.'s dogmatic employment;
And that, she averred, did mar her enjoyment.
She often had begged him to sell off his dogs
And instead to raise turkeys, spring chickens, or hogs.
She made him half promise at no distant day
He would sell the whole lot, not excepting old Tray;
And, as good luck would have it, but few days intervened
When, excepting old Tray's, every kennel was cleaned.
Ah, how his dear Dolly, with a voice glad and jolly,
Did soft-soap her dear for quitting his folly.
"And now, my dear J., please don't say me nay,
But the first opportunity sell also old Tray."
"I will my dear vrow, and I solemnly vow,
I'll give you the money to buy a good cow."
And thus the case rested, till one summer night
Her dear J. came home with a heart happy and light,
Old Tray was not with him. "Ah, ha, my good wife,
This will be far the happiest day of your life."
"Oh, bless you, dear J., how much did you say,
Please tell me at once what you got for old Tray?"
"I got forty dollars." "You did?" quoth his spouse,
"Why that to a certainty will buy me two cows,
I'll make butter and cheese"—"Hold on if you please"—
Says J. in a tone sounding much like a tease;

"It's just as I told you, the price is all right,
And the man is to pay me next Saturday night;
But instead of the dollar's in X's and V's,
He gives me four puppies at ten dollars apiece."

THE SMACK IN SCHOOL.

PALMER.

A DISTRICT school, not far away,
'Mid Berkshire hills, one winter's day.
Was humming with its wonted noise
Of three-score mingled girls and boys;
Some few upon their tasks intent,
But more on furtive mischief bent.
The while the master's downward look
Was fastened on a copy-book;
When suddenly, behind his back,
Rose sharp and clear a rousing smack!
As 'twere a battery of bliss
Let off in one tremendous kiss!
"What's that?" the startled master cries;
"That, thir," a little imp replies,
"Wath William Willith, if you pleathe—
I thaw him kith Thuthanna Peathe!"
With frown to make a statue thrill,
The master thundered, "Hither, Will!"
Like wretch o'ertaken in his track,
With stolen chattels on his back,
Will hung his head in fear and shame,
And to the awful presence came—
A great, green, bashful simpleton,
The butt of all good-natured fun.
With smile suppressed, and birch upraised,
The threatener faltered—"I'm amazed
That you, my biggest pupil, should
Be guilty of an act so rude!
Before the whole set school to boot—
What evil genius put you to't?"

" 'Twas she, herself, sir," sobbed the lad,
" I did not mean to be so bad;
But when Susannah shook her curls,
And whispered, I was 'fraid of girls,
And dursn't kiss a baby's doll,
I couldn't stand it, sir, at all,
But up and kissed her on the spot!
I know—boo-hoo—I ought to kot,
But, somehow, from her looks—boo-hoo—
I thought she kind o' wished me to!"

THE TINKER AND MILLER'S DAUGHTER.

WOLCOT.

THE meanest creature somewhat may contain,
As Providence ne'er makes a thing in vain.

Upon a day, a poor and trav'ling tinker,
In Fortune's various tricks a constant thinker,
    Pass'd in some village near a miller's door,
Where lo! his eye did most astonish'd catch
The miller's daughter peeping o'er the hatch,
Deform'd and monstrous ugly, to be sure.
Struck with the uncommon form, the tinker started,
Just like a frighten'd horse, or murd'rer carted,
    Up gazing at the gibbet and the rope;
Turning his brain about, in a brown study
(For, as I've said, his brain was not so muddy),
" Zounds!" quoth the tinker, " I have now some hope.
Fortune, the jade, is not far off, perchance,"
And then began to rub his hands and dance.

Now, all so full of love, o'erjoyed he ran,
Embraced and squeezed Miss Grist, and thus began:
    " My dear, my soul, my angel, sweet Miss Grist,
Now may I never mend a kettle more,
If ever I saw one like you before!"
    Then nothing loth, like Eve, the nymph he kiss'd.

Now, very sensibly, indeed, Miss Grist
Thought opportunity should not be miss'd;
Knowing that prudery oft let slip a joy;
Thus was Miss Grist too prudent to be coy.
For really 'tis with girls a dangerous farce
To flout a swain when offers are but scarce.
She did not scream, and cry, " I'll not be woo'd;
Keep off, you dingy fellow—don't be rude;
I'm fit for your superiors, tinker." No,
Indeed, she treated not the tinker so.
But lo! the damsel with her usual squint,
Suffered her tinker lover to imprint

Sweet kisses on her lips, and squeeze her hand,
Hug her, and say the softest things unto her,
And in love's plain and pretty language woo her,

Without a frown, or even a reprimand.

Soon won, the nymph agreed to be his wife,
And, when the tinker chose, to be tied for life.

Now, to the father the brisk lover hied,
Who at his noisy mill so busy plied,
Grinding, and taking handsome toll of corn,
Sometimes, indeed, too handsome to be borne.
" Ho! Master Miller," did the tinker say—

Forth from his cloud of flour the miller came;
" Nice weather, Master Miller—charming day—

Heaven's very kind." The miller said the same.
" Now, miller, possibly you may not guess

At this same business I am come about:
'Tis this, then—know I love your daughter Bess;—

There Master Miller!—now the riddle's out.
I'm not for mincing matters, sir! d'ye see—
I like your daughter Bess, and she likes me."

" Poh!" quoth the miller, grinning at the tinker,

" Thou dost not mean to marriage to persuade her;
Ugly as is old Nick, I needs must think her,

Though, to be sure, she is as heav'n has made her.
No, no, though she's my daughter, I'm not blind;

But, tinker, what hath now possessed thy mind:
Thou'rt the first offer she has met, by dad—
But tell me, tinker, art thou drunk or mad ? "
" No—I'm not drunk nor mad," the tinker cried,
" But Bet's the maid I wish to make my bride;
   No girl in these two eyes doth Bet excel.'
" Why, fool ! " the miller said, " Bet hath a hump !
And then her nose !—the nose of my old pump."

   "I know it," quoth the tinker, " know it well."
" Her face," quoth Grist, " is freckled, wrinkled, flat;
Her mouth as wide as that of my tom cat ;
   And then she squints a thousand ways at once—
Her waist a corkscrew; and her hair how red !
A downright bunch of carrots on her head—
   Why, what the deuce is got into thy sconce ? "

" No deuce is in my sconce," rejoined the tinker ;
" But, sir, what's that to you, if fine I think her ? "
" Why, man," quoth Grist, " she's fit to make a show,
   And therefore sure I am that thou must banter."
" Miller," replied the tinker, " right, for know
   'Tis for that very thing, a show, I want her."

AN ORIGINAL PARODY.

ANONYMOUS.

It must be so ! stomach thou reasonest well,
Else whence this pleasing hope, this fond desire ;
This longing after something good for dinner ?
Or whence these secret pangs ; these hollow murmurs,
That issue from my bowels ? Why shrinks my soul
Back on herself, and startles at a famine ?
'Tis hunger, powerful hunger, stirs within me ;
'Tis famine's self that points to *one o'clock* !
And shows the time of dinner is at hand.
Dinner ! thou pleasing, thou delightful thought,
Thro' what a variety of knowing processes,
Each morsel, both of lean and fat. doth pass,

Ere dinner, in rich prospect, lies before me,
And I with ardent stomach fall upon it.
Here will I hold! If Molly's in the kitchen,
And that she is, and in a bustle too,
Both nose and ears confess—she must be cooking something!
And that which Molly cooks, it must be tasty;
But when or where this dinner will be ready,
I'm weary of conjectures. Oh, patience, end them.
Thus am I wholly arm'd from top to toe,
Patience and appetite both working within me,
That gently bids me wait till I am called.
But this supposes I shall never dine;
The soul secure in her existence, smiles
At the debates, and thinks my stomach mad;
The kitchen fire shall fade, cookery itself
Grow out of date with mayors, and sauces be no more;
But thou shalt flourish in immortal youth—
Unhurt amid the war of pots and pans,
The wreck of gridirons and the crush of kitchens

THE PARSONS AND THE CORKSCREW.

MONCRIEFF.

Twelve parsons once went to a squire's to dine,
Who was famous for giving good venison and wine,
All great friends to *the cloth*, with *good living* in view,
Quite *grace full* they sat down, as parsons should do.
A wicked young whipster, our worthy squire's cousin,
Whispered, " Cousin, I boldly will lay rump and dozen,
Though here we've a dozen staunch priests, of the lot
Not one of the twelve here a prayer-book has got."
"Agreed," cried the squire. " Coz, we must not be loth
Such a wager to lay for the sake of the cloth.
The parsons, no doubt, to confute you are able,
So we'll bring, with the dinner, the bet on the table."
Dinner served; cried the squire, " A new grace I will say,
Has any one here got a prayer-book, I pray?"
Quite glum looked the priests, coughed, and with one accord

Cried " Mine's lost "—" Mine's at home "—" Mine's at church,
    'pon my word."
Quoth our cousin, " Dear squire, I my wager have won,
But another I purpose to win ere I've done ;
Though the parsons could not bring a prayer-book to view,
I'll bet the same bet, they can find a corkscrew."
" Done ! done ! " roared the squire. " Hilloa ! butler, bring
    nearer
That excellent magnum of ancient Madeira ; "
'Twas brought—" Let's *decant* it ; a corkscrew, good John."
Here *each* of the parsons roared out " *I've got one !* "
But let us not censure our parsons for this,
When a thing's in its place, it can ne'er come amiss ;
Prayer-books wont serve for corkscrews ; and I'm such a sinner,
Though a sermon I like, I don't want it at dinner !

THE OLD GENTLEMAN WHO MARRIED A YOUNG WIFE.

From the " School of Scandal."

SHERIDAN.

Characters.

SIR PETER TEAZLE.   LADY TEAZLE.

SIR PETER. Lady Teazle, Lady Teazle, I'll not bear it.

LADY T. Sir Peter, Sir Peter, you may bear it or not, as
you please; but I ought to have my own way in everything; and what's more, I will, too. What, though I was
educated in the country, I know very well that women of
fashion in London are accountable to nobody after they are
married.

SIR P. Very well, ma'am, very well! so, a husband is to
have no influence, no authority ?

LADY. T. Authority ! no, to be sure; if you wanted authority over me, you should have adopted me, and not married me. I am sure you were old enough.

SIR P. Old enough, aye, there it is. Well, well, Lady

Teazle, though my life may be made unhappy by your temper, I'll not be ruined by your extravagance.

LADY T. My extravagance! I'm sure I'm not more ex-
travagant than a woman of fashion ought to be.

SIR P. No, no, madam, you shall throw away no more
sums on such unmeaning luxury. 'Slife! to spend as much
to furnish your dressing-room with flowers in winter, as
would suffice to turn the Pantheon into a green-house, and
give a *fête champêtre* at Christmas.

LADY T. Lord, Sir Peter, am I to blame, because flowers
are dear in cold weather? you should find fault with the
climate and not with me. For my part, I'm sure, I wish it
were spring all the year round, and that roses grew under
our feet.

SIR P. Oons! madam, if you had been born to this, I
shouldn't wonder at your talking thus; but you forget what
your situation was when I married you.

LADY T. No, no, I don't; 'twas a very disagreeable one,
or I should never have married you.

SIR P. Yes, yes, madam, you were then in somewhat an
humble style; the daughter of a plain country 'squire.
Recollect, Lady Teazle, when I first saw you sitting at your
tambour, in a pretty figured linen gown, with a bunch of
keys at your side; your hair combed smooth over a roll, and
your apartment hung round with fruits in worsted, of your
own working.

LADY T. Oh, yes! I remember it very well, and a curious life I led. My daily occupation, to inspect the dairy,
superintend the poultry, make extracts from the family re-
ceipt-book, and comb my aunt Deborah's lap-dog.

SIR P. Yes, yes, madam, 'twas so, indeed.

LADY T. And then, you know, my evening amusements.
To draw patterns for ruffles, which I had not materials to
make up; to play Pope Joan with the curate; to read a
novel to my aunt; or to be stuck down to an old spinet to
strum my father to sleep after a fox-chase.

SIR P. I am glad you have got so good a memory. Yes,

madam, these were the recreations I took you from; but now you must have your coach, vis-à-vis, and three powdered footmen before your chair; and in the summer, a pair of white cats to draw you to Kensington Gardens. No recollection, I suppose, when you were content to ride double, behind the butler, on a dock'd coach-horse?

LADY T. No; I swear I never did that; I deny the butler and the coach-horse.

SIR P. This, madam, was your situation; and what have I done for you? I have made you a woman of fashion, of fortune, of rank; in short, I have made you my wife.

LADY T. Well, then, and there is but one thing more you can make me to add to the obligation, and that is—

SIR P. My widow, I suppose?

LADY T. Hem! hem!

SIR P. I thank you, madam; but don't flatter yourself; for though your ill conduct may disturb my peace of mind, it shall never break my heart, I promise you; however, I am equally obliged to you for the hint.

LADY T. Then why will you endeavor to make yourself so disagreeable to me, and thwart me in every little elegant expense.

SIR P. 'Slife, madam, I say, had you any of these little elegant expenses when you married me?

LADY T. Lud, Sir Peter! would you have me out of the fashion?

SIR P. The fashion, indeed! What had you to do with the fashion before you married me?

LADY T. For my part, I should think you would like to have your wife thought a woman of taste.

SIR P. Ay, there again; taste! zounds, madam, you had no taste when you married me.

LADY T. That's very true, indeed, Sir Peter; and after having married you, I should never pretend to taste again, I allow. But now, Sir Peter, since we have finished our daily jangle, I presume I may go to my engagement at Lady Sneerwell's.

SIR P. Ay, there's another precious circumstance ; a charming set of acquaintance you have made there.

LADY T. Nay, Sir Peter, they are all people of rank and fortune, and remarkably tenacious of reputation.

SIR P. Yes, egad, they are tenacious of reputation with a vengeance; for they don't choose anybody should have a character but themselves. Such a crew. Ah! many a wretch has rid on a hurdle who has done less mischief than these utterers of forged tales, coiners of scandal, and clippers of reputation.

LADY T. What! would you restrain the freedom of speech ?

SIR P. Ah, they have made you just as bad as any one of the society.

· LADY T. Why, I believe I do bear a part with tolerable grace.

SIR P. Grace, indeed!

LADY T. But I vow I bear no malice against the people I abuse. When I say an ill-natured thing, 'tis out of pure good humor ; and I take it for granted, they deal exactly in the same manner with me. But, Sir Peter, you know you promised to come to Lady Sneerwell's too.

SIR P. Well, well, I'll call in just to look after my own character.

LADY T. Then, indeed, you must make haste after me, or you'll be too late. So, good bye.   [*Exit.*

SIR P. So, I have gained much by my expostulations ; yet, with what a charming air she contradicts everything I say, and how pleasingly she shows her contempt for my authority. Well, though I can't make her love me, there is great satisfaction in quarrelling with her ; and I think she never appears to such advantage as when she is doing everything in her power to plague me.

CURTAIN.

THE STAGE-STRUCK DARKEY.

AN ETHIOPIAN INTERLUDE.

WHITE.

Scene.—*Street.*

Three or four PERFORMERS *seated on Stage. Enter* TRAVELLING MANAGER, *with valise, overcoat, &c.*

MANAGER. How do you do? Does any ob you folks want a situation?

ALL. What to do?

MANAGER. Well, I'm a travelling manager of a show and in search of talent. I want a young man of good natural parts, and I'll teach him de rest.

ALL. (*Speaking together.*) Julius is de berry boy.

Enter JULIUS, *whistling, and sauntering along.*

MANAGER. Young man, would you like to be an actor?

JULIUS. A what?

MANAGER. Have you ever been on de stage?

JULIUS. No, but I've drove three months on de Sixth Avenue cars.

MANAGER. Oh, you don't understand. See, look here. (*Strikes very tragic position.*) See—don't you see?

JULIUS. Yes, siree sir; I'm one ob dem.

MANAGER. Well, now I want a specimin to see what you're made of; I want to hear your voice. Suppose you touch me on de shoulder and call me a liar, as they do in anger on de stage.

JULIUS. It's a go—I'll do it. (*Walks around stage, then goes behind* MANAGER'S *back, slaps him on shoulder, and says, very faintly.*) Liar!

MANAGER. Oh, dat's too weak. Now let me show you. (*They change positions—*MANAGER *says, very savagely*) Liar-r-r-r-r' (*Waving body to and fro.*)

JULIUS. Why, what do you call dat? (*Imitating him.*)

MANAGER. Why, dat's your tragedy—don't you see?—and here's when you recover. (*Moving to and fro.*)

JULIUS. Well, what's next?

MANAGER. Let's see. What shall we play? Oh! something of our own? Yes; well, you play a man dat's been bery rich—you used to eat canvas-back ducks, an all dat arrangements; you libed in a castle on top ob a hill. (*Aside.*) Castles in de air. (*Aloud.*) An you owned a yacht, an used to gib balls, an all dat sort ob things. In short, you was a millionaire. Well, time wore on—you had a deal ob money invested in stocks; stocks went down, and you went up in a balloon; an now that you are a bankrupt, your daughter married a coachman, an den you've gone in altogeder. Dere, dat's your part. Now what shall I be? (*Thinks.*) I'll be a man dat was bery poor when you war so rich; you wouldn't look at me—no, siree, you wouldn't gib me de crumbs that fell from your table, no sir. Well, while you been gettin poor, I'be been to California, and made loads ob money; I'm coming home wid all dis money in dis casket, an you are driven to de highway. Your children haven't eat anything for six weeks, an you haven't eat anything for longer dan dat. You see me coming, an go an hide yourself till I come in; den you come forward, and try to bully and rob me; but you find dat won't do, so you try de pathetic; den I tell you to take de casket. I'll say, "Take it," but you mustn't take it de fust time; mind, de second time is your cue. Now let's see how you can play a starvin' man. (JULIUS *goes off, and comes on very fiercely, &c.*) Well, dat's a good gait for a blacksmith goin' to dinner, but remember, you haven't eat anything for—how long did I say?

JULIUS. Six weeks.

MANAGER. Well now, I'll show you how to walk. (*Comes forward, very shakily, C., and sighs.*)

JULIUS. What's dat for?

MANAGER. Why, dat's your sigh—don't you see? Mind, don't forget to keep up your shake. Try it again. (JULIUS *imitates* MANAGER *well.*) Now den for de road scene. (*Both exit —stage dark.*)

Enter JULIUS, *disguised.*

JULIUS. Ah me! For six weeks we have not tasted food.

Aha! what do I see ? As I live, a traveller comes dis way.
I'll hide an reconnoitre. (*Hides.*)

Enter MANAGER, *disguised genteelly, with casket.*

MANAGER. Haha! I am near my journey's end, methinks.
Old recollections crowd upon my brain, and—what ho!
(JULIUS *slaps him on the back.*) Hah!

JULIUS. Marry, I should know dat form.

MANAGER. Ha! dat face! 'Tis—*Keep up your shake!*

JULIUS. Rinaldo.

MANAGER. Rinaldo! *Keep up your shake!*

JULIUS. Aye, Rinaldo. Come, dis is no time for trifling.
You behold before you, or behind you, a desperate man,
driven to desperation by starvation. My wife and children
have eat no food for six weeks.

MANAGER. (*Aside.*) *Keep up your shake.*

JULIUS. I would have gold, gold—ha! ha!—gold!
Peaceably if I can, forcibly if I must. (*Seizes* MANAGER *by
the throat and chokes him*—MANAGER *kneels down.*) How's dat ?
Pooty good ?

MANAGER. (*Coughing.*) Well, pooty fair, but don't squeeze
quite so tight.

JULIUS. (*Rises.*) Dost scorn my threat?

MANAGER. Aye! thee and thy threat!

JULIUS. Behold me at thy feet—(*kneels*) me, Rinaldo, who
never bent nor bowed before created man. Relieve my wife
and starving children, and I am your slave forever.

MANAGER. Rise, Rinaldo. You shall have gold. Here,
take de casket. (JULIUS *makes grab at the casket, and each pull,
both take stage.*) Dere I knew you would spoil de piece.
Didn't I say de *second* time, take it ?

JULIUS. (*Angry at himself.*) Well, I didn't mean to do it
I thort you said de first time.

MANAGER. You'll neber make an actor. [*Exit.*

CURTAIN.

GOODY GRIM *VERSUS* LAPSTONE.

MATTHEWS.

JUDGE. (*Standing.*) What a profound study is THE LAW! and how difficult to fathom ! Well, let us consider the law, for our laws are very considerable, both in bulk and num bers, according as the statutes declare ; *considerandi, consider. ando, considerandum*, and are not to be meddled with by those who don't understand them.

Law always expresses itself with true grammatical pre· cision, never confounding moods, cases, or genders, except, indeed, when a woman happens accidentally to be slain, then a verdict is always brought in manslaughter. The essence of the law is altercation, for the law can altercate, fulminate, deprecate, irritate, and go on at any rate. " Your son follows the law, I think, Sir Thomas ? " " Yes, madam ; but I am afraid he will never overtake it ; a man following the law is like two boys running round a table; he follows the law, and the law follows him. However, if you take away the whereofs, whereases, wherefores, and notwithstandings, the whole mystery vanishes ; it is then plain and simple." Now, the quintessence of the law has, according to its name, five parts. The first is the beginning, or *incipiendum ;* the second, the uncertainty, or *dubitandum ;* the third, delay, or *puzzleendum ;* fourthly, replication without *endum ;* and, fifthly, *monstrum et hoverendum ;* all which is clearly exemplified in the following case— *Goody Grim against Lapstone.* This trial is as follows :—Goody Grim inhabits an almshouse, No. 2 ; Will Lapstone, a superannuated cobbler, in· habits No. 3 ; and a certain Jew peddler, who happened to pass through the town where those almshouses are situated, could only think of No. 1. Goody Grim was in the act of killing one of her own proper pigs, but the animal, disliking the ceremony, burst from her hold, ran through the semicir-· cular legs of the aforesaid Jew, knocked him in the mud, ran back to Will Lapstone's, the cobbler, upset a quart bot·

.tle full of gin, belonging to the said Lapstone, and took refuge in the cobbler's state bed.

The parties being, of course, in the most opulent circumstanoes, consulted counsel learned in the law. The result was, that Goody Grim was determined to bring an action against Lapstone, for the loss of her pig with a curly tail; and Lapstone to bring an action against Goody Grim, for the loss of a quart bottle full of Holland gin ; and Mordecai to bring an action against them both, for the loss of a tee-totum, that fell out of his pocket in the rencounter. They all delivered their briefs to counsel, before it was considered they were all parties and no witnesses. But Goody Grim, like a wise old lady as she is, now changed her battery, and is determined to bring an action against Lapstone, and bind over Mordecai as an evidence.

The indictment sets forth (*reads from paper*) " that he, Lapstone, not having the fear of the assizes before his eyes, but being moved by pig, and instigated by pruinsence, did, on the first day of April, a day sacred in the annals of the law, steal, pocket, hide and crib divers, that is to say, five hundred hogs, sows, boars, pigs and porkers, with curly tails, and did secrete the said five hundred hogs, sows, boars, pigs and porkers, with curly tails, in said Lapstone's bed, against the peace of our Lord the King, his crown and dignity."

Mordecai will be examined by Counsellor Puzzle. (*The Judge seats himself.*)

PUZZLE. Well, sir, what are you ?

MORDECAI. I sells old clo's, and sealing-wax, and puckles.

PUZZLE. I did not ask you what you sold ; I ask you what you are ?

MORDECAI. I am about five-and-forty.

PUZZLE. I did not ask your age ; I ask you what you are ?

MORDECAI. I am a Jew.

PUZZLE. Why couldn't you tell me that at first ? Well, then, if you are a Jew, tell me what you know of this affair.

MORDECAI. As I vas valking along—

PUZZLE. Man, I didn't want to know where you were walking.

MORDECAI. Vel, as I was valking along—

PUZZLE. So you will walk along, in spite of all that can be said.

MORDECAI. Pless ma heart, you frighten me out of my vits—as I vas valking along, I seed de unclean animal coming towards me, and so says I—Oh! Father Abraham, says I—

PUZZLE. Father Abraham is no evidence.

MORDECAI. You must let me tell my story my own vay, or I cannot tell it at all. As I vas valking along, I seed the unclean animal coming toward me, and he runn'd between my legs, and upshet me in te mut.

PUZZLE. Now, do you mean to say, upon your oath, that that little animal had the power to upset you in the mud?

MORDECAI. I vill take my oath dat he upshet me in te mut.

PUZZLE. And pray, sir, on what side did you fall?

MORDECAI. On te mutty side.

PUZZLE. I mean, on which of your own sides did you fall?

MORDECAI. I fell on my left side.

PUZZLE. Now, on your oath, was it on your left side?

MORDECAI. I vill take my oath it vas my left side.

PUZZLE. And pray, what did you do when you fell down?

MORDECAI. I got up again as fast as I could.

PUZZLE. Perhaps you can tell me whether the pig had a curly tail?

MORDECAI. I vill take ma oath his tail vas so curly as my peerd.

PUZZLE. And pray, where were you going when this happened?

MORDECAI. I vas going to de sign of de Cock and Pottle.

PUZZLE. Now, on your oath, what had a cock to do with a bottle?

MORDECAI. I don't know; only it vas the sign of de

house. And all more vat I know vas, dat I lose an ivory tee-totum out of ma pocket.

Puzzle. Oh, you lost a tee-totum, did you? I thought we should bring you to something at last. My Lord, I beg leave to take an exception to this man's evidence! he does not come into court with clean hands.

Mordecai. How te devil should I, when I have been polishing ma goods all morning?

Puzzle. Now, my Lord, your Lordship is aware that tee-totum is derived from the Latin terms *te* and *tutum*, which means " Keep yourself safe." And this man, but for my sagacity, observation, and so forth, would have kept himself safe; but now he has, as the learned Lord Verulam expresses it, " let the cat out of the bag."

Mordecai. I vill take ma oath " I had no cat in ma bag,"

Puzzle. My Lord, by his own confession he was about to vend a tee-totum. Now, my Lord, and gentlemen of the jury, it is my duty to point out to you that a tee-totum is an unlawful machine, made of ivory, with letters printed upon it, for the purpose of gambling. Now your Lordship knows the act commonly known by the name of " Little go Act," expressly forbids all games of chance whatever, whether put, whist, marbles, swabs, tee-totum, chuck - farthing, dumps, or what not. And therefore, I do contend that the man's evidence is *contra bonos mores*, and he is consequently *non compos testimonæ*.

Judge. Counsellor Botherem will now proceed.

Botherem My Lord, and gentlemen of the jury, my learned friend Puzzle has, in a most facetious manner, endeavored to cast a slur on the highly honorable evidence of the Jew merchant. And I do contend that he who buys and sells is *bona-fide* inducted into all the mysteries of merchandise ; ergo, he who merchandises is, to all intents and purposes, a merchant. My learned friend, in the twistings and turnings of his argument in handling the tee-totum, can only be called *obiter dictum ;* he is playing, my Lord, a losing game. Gentlemen, he has told you the origin, use, and abuse, of the tee-totum ; but, gentlemen, he has forgot to tell you what that great luminary of the law, the late learned Coke, has said on the subject, in a case exactly similar to this, in the 234th folio volume of the Abridgment of the Statutes, page 1349, where he thus lays down the law in the case of Hazard *versus* Blacklegs : "*Gamblendum consistet, enac!- um gamblendi, sed non evendum macheni playendi*." My Lord, I beg leave to say that, if I prove my client was in the act of vending, and not playing, with the said instrument, the tee-totum, I humbly presume that all my learned friend has said will come to the ground.

JUDGE. Certainly, brother Botherem, there's no doubt the learned Sergeant is incorrect. The law does not put a man *extralegium* for merely spinning a tee-totum.

BOTHEREM. My Lord, one of the witnesses has owned that the pig had a curly tail. Now, my Lord, I presume if I prove the pig had a straight tail, I consider the ob. jection must be fatal.

JUDGE. Certainly : order the pig into court. (*The pig being produced, upon examination, is found to have a straight tail.*)

In summing up the evidence, gentlemen of the jury, it is wholly unnecessary to recapitulate ; for the removal of this objection removes all ground of action. And notwithstanding the ancient statute, which says *Serium pigum et boreum pigum, et vendi curlum tailum,* there is an irrefragable proof, by ocular demonstration, that Goody Grim's grunter has a straight tail ; and, as it has been distinctly proved that the pig set forth in the indictment had a curly tail, it is evident that it was somebody else's pig ; *ergo,* it was not Goody Grim's pig at all, and therefore the prisoner must be acquitted. And really, gentlemen, if the time of the court is to be taken up with these frivolous actions, the designs of justice will be entirely frustrated ; and the attorney who recommends this action should be punished, not in the ordinary way, but with the utmost rigor and severity of the law

THE WOMAN OF MIND.

ANONYMOUS.

MY wife is a woman of mind,
  And Deville, who examined her bumps,
Vowed that never was found in a woman
  Such large intellectual lumps.
" Ideality " big as an egg,
  With "Causality "—great—was combined;
He charged me ten shillings, and said,
  "Sir, your wife is a woman of mind."

She's too clever to care how she looks,
  And will horrid blue spectacles wear,
Not because she supposes they give her
  A fine intellectual air ;
No ! she pays no regard to appearance,
  And combs all her front hair behind,
Not because she is proud of her forehead,
  But because she's a woman of mind.

She makes me a bushel of verses,
  But never a pudding or tart,
If I hint I should like one, she vows
  I'm an animal merely at heart;
Though I've noticed she spurns not the pastry,
  Whene'er at a friend's we have dined,
And has always had two plates of pudding—
  Such plates! for a woman of mind.

Not a stitch does she do but a distich,
  Mends her pens, too, instead of my clothes;
I haven't a shirt with a button,
  Nor a stocking that's sound at the toes ;
If I ask her to darn me a pair,
  She replies she has work more refined;
Besides to be seen darning stockings !
  Is it fit for a woman of mind ?

The children are squalling all day,
  For they're left to the care of a maid;
My wife can't attend to " the units,"
  " The millions " are wanting her aid,
And it's vulgar to care for one s offspring—
  The mere brute ha; a love of its kind—
But *she* loves the whole human fam'ly,
  For *she* is a woman of mind.

Everything is an inch thick in dust,
  And the servants do just as they please
The ceilings are covered with cobwebs,
  The beds are all swarming with fleas;
The windows have never been clean'd,
  And as black as your hat is each blind;
But my wife's nobler things to attend to,
  For she is a woman of mind.

The nurse steals the tea and the sugar,
  The cook sells the candles as grease,
And gives all the cold meat away
  To her lover who's in the police;
When I hint that the housekeeping's heavy,
  And hard is the money to find,
" Money's vile filthy dross!" she declares,
  And unworthy a woman of mind.

Whene'er she goes out to a dance,
  She refuses to join in the measure,
For dancing she can't but regard
  As an unintellectual pleasure.
So she gives herself up to enjoyments
  Of a more philosophical kind,
And picks all the people to pieces,
  Like a regular woman of mind.

She speaks of her favorite authors
  In terms far from pleasant to hear;
" Charles Dickens " she vows " is a darling,"
  " And Bulwer " she says " is a dear; "

" Wilkie Collins " with her " is an angel,"
   And I'm an " illiterate hind."
Upon whom her fine intellect s wasted,
   I'm not fit for a woman of mind.

She goes not to church on a Sunday,
   Church is all very well in its way,
But she is too highly informed
   Not to know all the parson can say ;
It does well enough for the servants,
   And was for poor people designed,
But bless you ! it's no good to her,
   For she is a woman of mind.

NURSERY REMINISCENCES.

BARHAM.

I remember, I remember,
   When I was a little boy,
One fine morning in September
   Uncle brought me home a toy.

I remember how he patted
   Both my cheeks in kindliest mood ;
" There," said he, " you little fat head,
   There's a top because you're good."

Grandmamma—a shrewd observer—
   I remember gazed upon
My new top, and said with fervor,
   " Oh, how kind of Uncle John ! "

While mamma, my form caressing—
   In her eye the tear-drop stood—
Read me this fine moral lesson,
   " See what comes of being good ! "

I remember, I remember,
  On a wet and windy day,
One cold morning in December,
  I stole out and went to play;

I remember Billy Hawkins
  Came, and with his pewter squirt
Squibb'd my pantaloons and stockings,
  Till they were all over dirt!

To my mother for protection
  I ran—quaking every limb—
She exclaimed, with fond affection,
  " Gracious goodness! look at him!"

Pa cried, when he saw my garment—
  'Twas a newly-purchased dress—
" Oh! you nasty little warment,
  How came you in such a mess?"

Then he caught me by the collar—
  Cruel only to be kind—
And to my exceeding dolor,
  Gave me—several slaps behind.

Grandmamma, while yet I smarted,
  As she saw my evil plight,
Said—'twas rather strong-hearted—
  " Little rascal! sarve him right!"

I remember, I remember,
  From that sad and solemn day,
Never more in dark December
  Did I venture out to play.

And the moral which they taught, I
  Well remember; thus they said—
"Little boys, when they are naughty,
  Must be whipped and sent to bed!"

A MARTYR TO SCIENCE; OR, WANTED—A CONFEDERATE.

AN ORIGINAL FARCE, IN ONE ACT, FOR MALE CHARACTERS ONLY.

F. WESTON.

Characters.

TWEEZER, *a retired Chiropodist, aged* 60.
DICK, *his son, aged* 25.
HUMPHREY DAVY RATTLETON, A.B.C.D.E.F., &c., &c., &c.,
Peripatetic Lecturer on Magnetico-photographico-biology, aged 30.
DRUDGLEY, *a Lawyer, aged* 50.

SCENE—*Tweezerville, near New York.*

TIME—*The present.*

COSTUMES—*Of the day.*

SCENE—*A room comfortably, and rather gaudily furnished, a small table at* R., *a larger in the centre, chairs, a window opening to garden. Doors,* R. *and* L. (*For stage directions see page* 64)

TWEEZER (*Calls, without,* R.) Dick! Dick!

Enter TWEEZER, R.

TWEEZ. Out again! What a mania that boy has for agriculture! Ever since I bought this snug little box, in which I might rest my corns—no! I mean my bones, and enjoy a little quiet, Dick has devoted himself to rural affairs with an ardor which has quite surprised me; I don't believe he knew a rose from a dandelion when we lived in New York, and now, now he breaks my head with all sorts of Latin names for the most uncommon flowers. There's something more than flowers at the root of it; it isn't natural, this sudden and unusual devotion to such a simple pursuit as botany. I must take care he doesn't fall in love with the wrong woman—*that* would be a terrible mistake; old Jack Stilton and I have put our heads together; we agree that Letitia was made for Dick, Dick made for Letitia, and when

Jack and I *do* make up our minds about anything, it is not very easy to move us.

DICK *appears at open window.*

Ah, Dick! Where have you been since breakfast?

DICK. Studying botany, as usual, all among the lilies and daffadowndillies—charming pursuit! I can't say how much I love—the country. Who could live in town? Groves of chimneys, atmosphere of smoke, rivers of mud, not a glimpse of green fields, not a breath of pure air—

TWEEZ. But does it not occur to you, Dick, that without towns, we could hardly retire into the country? How did I make my money? not by growing my own corn, but by cutting other people's—and corns, Dick, are an institution of this great country—a civic institution, without which, I need hardly say, the vested rights of chiropodists would cease to be; how then could that most useful class live?

DICK. But surely, father, you don't wish me to follow that profession?

TWEEZ. By no means—by no means! no, you shall be a lawyer; you've the gift of talk, you have plenty of—cheek; and are by no means deficient in brains—in short, you're a chip of the old block; and so, as I made my money by the weakness of other people's understandings, you shall make yours by understanding their weakness.

DICK. Be it so. Though I shan't like goosequills as well as jonquils, nor think parchment as beautiful as a parterre; I must begin to do something for myself—I'm of age—and I must try to carve out a road to fortune.

TWEEZ. (*Aside.*) Now's the time to bring in a word of Letitia. (*Aloud.*) You're right, my dear boy, right—right—and I'll give you a reason for working, one you little dream of.

DICK. (*Aside.*) He doesn't mean a wife, surely.

TWEEZ. I'll tell you a secret, Dick—one that concerns yourself.

DICK. I'm all attention, father.

Tweez. When I first cut corns in New York, I began with a dollar in my pocket, and a brass plate on my door. Ah! that brass was a good investment, a little sometimes goes a long way. Little did I think, however, of once owning a villa in the country. I worked on, on, on—at last I married. She was a good woman if ever there was one.

Dick. Ah, sir! I never knew her.

Tweez. And my only grief now is, that she is not here to share with me the prosperity we dreamt of so far away. A wife, Dick, a wife is a great help.

Dick. (*Aside.*) I hardly can venture yet to tell him all. (*Aloud.*) A wife is—

Tweez. Who is that, Dick? (*Pointing off.*) Ah! Mr. Drudgley, my lawyer, he comes on a little matter of business—rather inconveniently at this moment, as I wished particularly to speak to you on a subject. Leave us, Dick; come back to luncheon.

Dick. (*Aside.*) Wants to get rid of me. (*Aloud.*) Oh! I can go and botanize for an hour. (*Aside.*) Dearest Emily! he must soon be told everything, My dear old dad will forgive me, but what will Emily's father say?

[*Exit at window.*

Drudg. (*Without.*) Don't trouble, I'll announce myself. (*Knocks.*)

Tweez. Come in!

Enter Drudgley, l. *door.*

Good morning, Mr. Drudgley, I had hardly expected to see you so soon.

Drudg. That, sir, is only because, in common with the world at large, you belie our profession. All the world is in a conspiracy (which I would indict if I could) to call the law dilatory. There certainly was a branch of the profession that was so, but with that I never meddled; Chancery has always been a proverb for delay; my line runs in another direction entirely.

Tweez. Well! then I may hope that you've brought the

papers relative to the mortgage. I do not conceal from you, Mr. Drudgley, that in thus investing a very large portion of what I possess, I am bound to be cautious, perhaps suspicious. I must cut down to the very root.

DRUDG. As you once did professionally in re Corn and Bunion versus Foot, eh? You're quite right, Mr. Tweezer; it would indeed be quite contrary to my mode of transacting business to allow clients to hurry themselves. Look into the matter, sir, till you see truth shining at the very bottom of the legal well. Ah! if every one of my clients always did that—if they only had a little of your caution, perhaps suspicion, as you call it, there would be little enough for us to do sometimes.

TWEEZ. Well! leave the papers with me—I've a quiet day. All the world but ourselves is gone to the races—I shall have no interruptions—

DRUDG. (*Consulting memorandum book.*) Is there a Miss Titmarsh residing hereabouts?—Emily Titmarsh?—living with her aunt, Mrs. Hobbleton.

TWEEZ. To be sure there is; not half a mile distant across the fields—go across my meadow—it will save you half the walk.

DRUDG. Thank you—thank you. Now read over the papers very carefully; with your acute intellect and business habits you'll have mastered the subject long before my return. [*Exit at window,* TWEEZER *giving him directions.*

TWEEZ. And now for a quiet investigation of my new venture. Drudgley represents to me that it must double the investment, and that the mortgage is sure to come into my hands; if so, Dick will be thoroughly well off, and with Jack Stilton's savings, the young couple will "do." I don't quite like Drudgley's excessively complimentary addresses. He always talks about my business habits; I must look with some—caution into the papers. Yet—isn't he right? I am a good man of business—have been so all my life. At all events, I've not signed yet. Now for it. (*As he begins to settle down to read, the gate bell rings.*) Now, in the name of all that's uncomfortable, who can this be ? Miss MacWheedle, I shouldn't wonder—that woman has a design on me I do believe.

RATTLETON. (*Without.*) Where is my friend ?

TWEEZ. A stranger. I don't know the voice.

RATTLE. Stand aside, nor hinder the embrace of friend-ship. (*Runs in a' L. door.*)

TWEEZ. This is some mistake—a stranger !

RATTLE. What do you mean by stranger ? Whas do you mean by mistake ? Ah ! you don't remember me—fortu-nately, *I* have a better memory. I remember *you* perfectly. Do you pretend to have forgotten that glorious day on board the excursion boat ? Ah ! Tweezer, Tweezer ! did we not vow eternal friendship ? Did I not see you home ? Did not you, with amiable pertinacity, planting your foot on your native—doormat, exclaim, Tweezer is not unmindful—none of his clan were ungrateful—

TWEEZ. I beg, sir—

RATTLE. To apologize ? no ! Say no more—confession is half way to restitution. Though you forget, I forgive ; and according to your polite and pressing invitation, here I am—you said—

TWEEZ. (*In despair.*) Sir—

RATTLE. I remember—thank you—that was the precise word with which you began. You said, "Sir, I shall ever retain a grateful and lively recollection of this day's scien-tific conversation." "Mr. Rattleton," you continued, " I do not hesitate to class you among the remarkable men of this age, and if ever "—This is the point—" if ever "—mind, if I don't quote you word for word, forgive me, " If ever you come near Tweezerville, without looking up old Dick Tweez-er, he'll never forgive you the slight." To-day it so happens that fate kindly brings me to this neighborhood. To my delighted eyes there appears on each side of a gate, painted in Romanesque capitals, " Tweezerville," and dear Dick Tweezer's name on a bright brass plate. (*With emotion.*) I could *not* bear that you should feel slighted—and so here I am. This is my carpet bag—and here, ready to strain you to his aching heart, stands your friend—prepared to accept your hospitality, and (at a future date) to return it.

TWEEZ. Now, sir, that you have expended your super-fluous breath, allow *me* to speak. I do not at all remember the affair of the excursion boat, or the scientific conversation, or any pressing offer of hospitality, or even the *dear* friend **I** see so suddenly before me.

RATTLE. Well, it's excusable!—we parted late. Confound the salmon; it gave even me a head-ache in the morning—would it were among the extinct animals of the museum!—but it did not obliterate from "this distracted globe" the great fact of the invitation. You don't dispute its being *given*, I hope?—you don't dispute its being accepted, I hope? So, I'm come to revel in a quiet, philosophical, scientific way —Ah! how seldom is it that we escape from our learned so-cieties at this season of the year!

TWEEZ. But *who* or *what* are you? My memory does not even serve to recall your face.

RATTLE. (*Aside.*) How should it?

TWEEZ. Favor me with the name of the gentleman who thus honors Tweezerville with his presence.

RATTLE. Now that's capitally acted! bravo! I shouldn't have thought you'd so much "go" in you. A quiet, de-mure old fellow like you! Ah! when we discussed ichthy-osauri on board the excursion boat, I had no idea that you could make so good a figure on the boards.

TWEEZ. Boards!—what boards?

RATTLE. The stage—Thespis—Melpomene—Thalia—all that sort of thing! But, seriously speaking, you *can't* have forgotten Humphrey Davy Rattleton—a man with a tail of initial letters as long as a luggage train, at present lectur-ing on the newly-discovered science of Magnetico-photo-graphico-biology, and about to enlighten on that subject the Institute in the next town. As the lecture comes off to-morrow night, your offer of a bed comes most oppor-tunely.

TWEEZ. Excuse me, sir, but the *offer* of a bed, as you are pleased to call it, has not been made.

RATTLE. The *bed* not made. Tell Mary Ann to air the sheets—I'm not afraid of damp beds *here !*

TWEEZ. I can hardly help laughing at his assurance—Sir, had you *written*, I should have been prepared to do honor to *my long expected guest ;* as it is, I can only wish you—

RATTLE. To accept temporary hospitality—good—

TWEEZ. And now, Mr. Rattlepate—

RATTLE. Rattleton, if you please—I'm rather particular about my name—it does not signify just at present, but a good deal of money *might* depend on the manner of spelling it—*might* depend—hem ! I say nothing.

TWEEZ. Well, Mr. Rattleton—then—

RATTLE. Stay ! Stand as you are. What a study for a painter !—benevolence—hospitality—humor—all largely—*very* largely developed. Let me prevail on you to come over and hear me lecture to-morrow night—nay ; even to assist me in my experiments—in the name of science, I implore you. I have never had a favorable example yet—you present that example—I shall succeed with you, I know. (*Aside.*) He'd be a glorious confederate—known and respected in the neighborhood. (*Aloud.*) Come—say you'll come. I shall demonstrate the science of magnetic fluids generally ; and you—you are a whole battery in yourself—scientific—

TWEEZ. I beg your pardon, sir—I am a very plain and unscientific person.

RATTLE. Excuse me there. Every line in your face belies that statement—science is in every wrinkle—not fully developed—no—but the material is there. The mine is no less a mine, because the spade and mattock have left the soil virgin still. The ore is there, sir, though the hum of labor has never yet disturbed the holy calm of nature. (*Aside.*) *I must* have him—and such a confederate is not to be had every day.

TWEEZ. I can only repeat, sir, that I have no magnetism, and no other *ism* about me : that I know nothing, and care nothing about *ologies* of any sort, and am altogether unscien. tific.

RATTLE. Really, Tweezer, this is provoking. I've never thoroughly succeeded yet, for want of—of—an assistant— furnished with magnetic fluid, as I see you are, and willing to give way to the influences of the lecturer.

TWEEZ. In plain words—a confederate. Sir, you've come down here on false pretences—you've—

RATTLE. Take your time, Tweezer—Listen to me while you recover your breath. We magnetico-photographico-biologists are benefactors to the human race; but the ignorant world is against us. Now, *our* fluids—yours and mine —are in accord—with *you*, I should succeed—I know I should.

TWEEZ. But I'm not a fluid.

RATTLE. Yes, you are—that's the curious thing about it. I never noticed it on board the excursion boat, but you *are* one huge battery of magnetic fluid; and you must help me, call yourself what you will—assistant, illustrator, even confederate—I'll not quarrel about words; lend me half-a-dollar.

TWEEZ. I?

RATTLE. Yes! just for an experiment. I left my purse at home, and metal is essential.

TWEEZ. Well, here is one. You'll restore it, of course! (*Gives money.*)

RATTLE. Do you doubt me?

TWEEZ. Hem!

RATTLE. Now, let me explain. You gaze upon the coin which I hold thus—I pass my hands before you so—don't be alarmed—you can be persuaded to almost anything; when once I have you in accord with my fluid—

TWEEZ. Persuade me to almost anything? Perhaps persaude me to go to your lecture—

RATTLE. Anything. Only you must yield to my influence.

TWEEZ. It's quite demoniacal—if true. You say that you never succeeded yet.

RATTLE. Never; but then I hadn't found a good fluid. Now I have. Let us proceed. Would you like to know what people *think* about ?—the value of property—the state of their affections—

TWEEZ. Ah, yes—if I could—

RATTLE. You *can*, when once I place this coin thus—in the palm of my hand—you gaze on it—I proceed with my lecture—

TWEEZ. Let us hear what you have to say.

RATTLE. I'll cut all the first part of it, and come to the experiments. You'll always see the scientific people asleep at lectures, till we come to the experiments. Keep your eye on the half-dollar.

TWEEZ. That I will. (*Aside.*) Nothing shall tempt me to take my eyes off.

RATTLE. "Ladies and gentlemen—The gigantic science, of which I am but a humble votary, having been fully explained to you in the first part of this evening's address, it now becomes my pleasing duty to illustrate my remarks by a few experiments on individuals taken at random from the distinguished and intellectual body assembled in this hall." Hear! Hear!

TWEEZ. Who says that ?

RATTLE. The audience, to be sure—audiences always concur in observations complimentary to themselves. But don't interrupt—this highly respectable gentleman—that's you—

TWEEZ. Hear, hear!

RATTLE *You* mustn't say that—

TWEEZ. Oh! I thought you said we always concur in complimentary observations.

RATTLE. True, the audience does—this highly respectable gentleman—

TWEEZ. Hear, hear!

BATTLE. Silence—you put me out.

TWEEZ. (*Aside.*) I can't.

RATTLE. With whom I've not the slightest previous acquaintance—

TWEEZ. But you had—or how should I be there?

RATTLE. Thankye, Tweezer, for reminding me about the excursion boat. In public, however, we must not have any communication. For science to make way with the million, we must humbug a little. Don't interrupt—you keep looking at the half-dollar.

TWEEZ. Ah, that I do!

RATTLE. This person, selected at random from among yourselves, will allow me to pass the magnetic current through his system. See! I now proceed to deprive him of all distinct individuality. He becomes as it were a part of myself—he and I know each other's thoughts and wishes. I bid him sit down—See! he sits. Rise! he rises. Hold out the right arm—See! he does so. Be in a garden—smell the flowers. (TWEEZER *sniffs violently*.) Bravo!—now, Tweezer, you can do that?

TWEEZ. Of course, now that I am your fluid, I must do whatever you tell me.

RATTLE. Bravo! bravo! we should make a fortune together. I see a brilliant career of spirit-rapping—table-turning—invisible flights—a fortune! You'll come, and do this for me.

TWEEZ. I must—command your fluid!

RATTLE. Enough for the present Why, is it possible that I have succeeded? By Minerva! I have then. I hope I shall be able to undo my work. Does the effect really go off, as they say, in half-an-hour? (*Slips the half-dollar into his pocket.*)

TWEEZ. Hullo! that's my half-dollar.

RATTLE. To be sure it is. He's wide awake about that, at all events. Now, I must keep every one else out, at all events, till I relieve Tweezer from his trance. (*Locks the door.*) Ah, what do I see? That old shark, Drudgley, coming this way. He has at least one suit out against me. I must flit—he's coming towards the window—then the door must befriend me.   [*Unlocks door and exits,* L.

Enter DRUDGLEY *by window—meanwhile* TWEEZER, *under the influence of the magnetism, remains perfectly passive—the actor on each person touching his hand should acquire a sudden vitality and consciousness.*

DRUDGLEY. Well, Mr. Tweezer, have you read the papers, and mastered their contents? (*Pause.*) Is he deaf, I wonder! I say (*louder*), have you mastered the papers? Are you ready to sign? (*Pause.*) What, silent still? Very odd—sir— s¹r—I really begin to be alarmed. (*Takes his hand.*)

TWEEZ. So you've come back!

DRUDG. (*Drawing a long breath.*) What a relief! Why, I've been standing here talking to you for a minute or two, without getting any answer. I feared you were ill.

TWEEZ. And what answer do you expect to get? What answer do you deserve?

DRUDG. Deserve—*deserve*, Mr. Tweezer? Why, the answer of a true friend to a conscientious lawyer.

TWEEZ. Ah! if you were one.

DRUDG. What do you mean—do you wish to insult me?

TWEEZ. It's of no sort of use blustering—the mortgage is not worth the paper the deed's engrossed on.

DRUDG. (*Aside.*) Who can have been here? Not even a clerk knows for whom the mortgage was to be. (*Aloud.*) Mr. Tweezer, I don't understand such language from one who is under great obligations to me—I should not, sir, (*emotion*) I *could* not have expected this—I should as soon have looked for the wife of my bosom—

TWEEZ. Ha! ha! ha!

DRUDG. What do you mean? Is there anything ludicrous in a man quoting the opinion, or appealing to the experience of the women who must know him best of all the world? I should as soon expect Mrs. Drudgley to doubt my honor, as one who was once, at any rate, my valued client, and excellent friend. (*Appears overcome.*)

TWEEZ. Now, no crocodile tears; you know that Mrs. Drudgley is your master—the better horse, eh? People at large think you're head of the firm. *we* know better.

DRUDG. (*Aside.*) Has she been here? Impossible! she *said* she was going to her aunt's—aunts are convenient relations sometimes; she goes to see her because I will not have aunt Sally in my house, but I mustn't quarrel. (*Aloud.*) Ah! Mr. Tweezer, you always were fond of a joke.

TWEEZ. You call it a joke, do you? you're quite right to treat it as such, if *you* don't mind it, of course *I* don't.

DRUDG. (*Aside.*) I wish I knew how much he really knows; there certainly is something very wild—insanity or inebriation—in his eye. I must find the son, he'll be able to explain what's the matter with his father; I wonder if he is mad. [*Exit in alarm, window.*

TWEEZ. (*Calling after him.*) No, sir, Tweezer is not mad. He has recovered his senses. This is a capital thing, to learn what each one thinks and means. I *feel* Dick coming—but he's not clear—all in a mist. I shall not know what the mystery is till *my* fluid communicates with the pulsation of his. (*Sits down.*)

DICK *enters at door* L.

DICK. There sits my dad. Now for a confession. Father! (*Pause.*) Father! (*Pause.*) Why, what sudden deafness is this? The poor dear old boy isn't ill, I hope. (*Touches him.*)

TWEEZ. Ah, Dick! so you've been with Emily?

DICK. Emily, sir!

TWEEZ. Yes. You don't mean to pretend you haven't been there, do you?

DICK. Certainly not, as you say so. I've been with Emily! —how did he learn it? (*Aside.*)

TWEEZ. I hope you love her dearly?

DICK. Dearly, sir?—that I do. Bravo! this is the wife he mysteriously hinted at just now. We shall get on like a house on fire!

TWEEZ She's a good girl, I believe, Dick?

DICK. The best of girls, sir. I'm delighted that you approve of my choice.

TWEEZ. But I don't. I meant you to marry another— Letitia Stilton; not that I'd interfere with your affections.

But you should have consulted me before you proposed to Emily.

DICK. Why, we feared you might not give your consent; and so—and so—

TWEEZ. And so you did without it? and got married—

DICK. Married, sir? How on earth did you learn that we were married?—you didn't know it this morning, for you were on the point of opening the subject when Mr. Drudgley—Ah! of course, Drudgley—he's the intending mischief maker. But, fortunately for us, he has not succeeded in setting you against us.

TWEEZ. Drudgley knows nothing about it; never mind him. Let us make the best of what's done. We can't have bigamy even for Jack Stilton's daughter. But I ought to be very angry.

DICK. Forgive us this once; we'll never do it again. You'll see Emily—I know you'll like her—she'll idolize you. You'll call her daughter, won't you?

TWEEZ. Ah! but what will Jack Stilton say? He used to be *such* a fiery fellow. He used to beat the watchmen once—a long time ago : we got taken before Sir Richard Birnie—hem! Do you think he'll forgive Emily?

DICK. You must talk him over. The memory of your joint indiscretions in youth will mollify him. But *do* tell me how you learnt that we were married.

RATTLETON *enters cautiously at window.* TWEEZER, *who appears to move machanically, sinks in a chair.*

RATTLE. Coast clear? Father and son tête-à-tête, I suppose.

DICK. Ah! sir, is it you who have done me the favor of meddling in my private affairs? You have fortunately done no mischief, whatever you intended.

RATTLE. I've nothing to do with your private affairs. I don't know what you mean by mischief. I've made none. (*Aside.*) I conclude the old one has been enlightening him. Bravo the science of magnetico-photographico-biology.

DICK. I'm really much obliged to your officious zeal. You have opened a very delicate subject with my father. As it happens (no thanks to your intentions) he is quite willing to forgive my marriage with Emily Titmarsh.

RATTLE. Emily—Titmarsh! Say it again.

DICK Emily Titmarsh.

RATTLE. This is indeed a surprise—a very disagreeable surprise.

DICK. Confound it! you surely don't affect ignorance of my union with her? Yes, she is no longer a Titmarsh but a Tweezer!

RATTLE. This is indeed a blow! From this day forth let us never meet, for if we do, it must be as foes. I loved Emily.

DICK. Loved my wife!

RATTLE. No; she was to be my wife.

DICK. Impossible!

RATTLE. But true nevertheless. She did indeed reject me, but I lived in hopes. Those hopes you have dashed to the ground. Oh! Emily—false—false! Why was I born? Why do I live?

DICK. Don't be absurd; the days of heroics are over! I have won the lady. She's mine. I'm going now to bring her home.

RATTLE. Spare me that pang at least. Let me not look on her.

DICK. Pooh! pooh! Now, Emily, dear, you shall come to your future home. [*Exit* DICK, L. *door.*

RATTLE. Well! that's off my mind. I can't hope any more in that quarter. I can't have the niece. I'll try the aunt. She's got two thousand dollars a year I know, and all at her own disposal. Ah! Tweezer seems recovering himself.

TWEEZ. (*Rubbing his eyes, and resuming his natural manner.*) What! Mr. Rattleton, not gone, I thought you were to be at New York by this time.

RATTLE. We haven't lunched yet.

TWEEZ. Haven't we?—I've been dreaming, then. Where's my son, I wonder?

RATTLE. He was here just now; he's stepped out for a minute. Let me have some luncheon, and be off. But, never fear, I'll fetch you to-morrow, my cultivator of the humanities. I'll take the liberty of ringing the bell. (*Rings.*)

TWEEZ. You've done nothing but take liberties all the morning. (*Aside.*)

Enter SERVANT *at door,* L.

Lunch!   [*Exit* SERVANT—*returns with tray.*

RATTLE. (*Sits down to lunch.*) Your health, Tweezer. Capital sherry—very.

Enter DICK, L.

DICK. I forgot one thing—Why, here's this fellow making himself at home!

TWEEZ. Dick, I've something to say to you.

DICK. Looks grave! Can't be a lecture, after our amicable understanding just now.

TWEEZ. We were interrupted this morning. just as I was going to broach a very interesting subject.

DICK. Yes, sir; but since then we've said all that is necessary to be said, haven't we? I've great pleasure in remembering all the kind things you said. Though you *said* you were angry, I didn't believe you; your words were contradicted by your looks.

TWEEZ. What are you dreaming of?

DICK. I confess I did not expect to find you thought me old enough to marry—

TWEEZ. Not *old* enough? On the contrary, marriage is what I set my heart on.

DICK. So I found, to my great surprise. Well, sir, are we to live here for the present?

TWEEZ. It would be most convenient, perhaps; but there'll be time enough for all that when the preliminaries are settled.

DICK. I don't quite comprehend you. What sort of preliminaries do you mean?

TWEEZ. Why, my dear Dick, you know that however well the parents may understand one another, and however well the young people may understand one another, there are times and seasons—consent to be asked—the day fixed—the knot tied—

DICK. I'm all at sea.

TWEEZ. I'll bring you into port. Jack Stilton has only to be asked, and Letitia will be your own.

DICK. What can the governor be driving at? He knows I'm married to Emily, and wants me now to marry Letitia. Let us if we can, sir, get at something like an explanation.

RATTLE. (*Finishing his luncheon.*) Let me explain.

TWEEZ. You'd better not interfere, sir.

RATTLE. But I must interfere!—justice demands it!— your son already loves, but not the lady you destine for him.

TWEEZ. Not Letitia! Who then is his choice?

DICK. Oh, father!—to ask such a question after giving your consent to my marriage.

TWEEZ. What marriage? This is the first I've heard of it. What marriage?

DICK. My marriage with Emily.

TWEEZ. Your marriage with Emily?

RATTLE. His marriage with Emily!

DICK. I confessed this morning in this room, not an hour ago, that I was already a married man.

TWEEZ. Pinch me, somebody! Do you mean to say you're actually married to her?

DICK. Yes; and that you are quite ready to welcome her as a daughter.

TWEEZ. Not a word of truth in the whole story.

RATTLE. Oh, Tweezer! that salmon again—at one o'clock in the day too!—fie, fie!

TWEEZ. Do you want to drive me wild?

DICK. No, sir; but I want you to abide by your own words. I asked you how you had learnt that I was married.

you told me it didn't signify—nay, hear me out—that you would make the best of it and forgive us.

TWEEZ. You mean to persuade me that I forgave you! that I said all this! You'll persuade me that I am not myself soon.

RATTLE. Only beside yourself. I once loved Emily Titmarsh. She rejected me—I lost sight of her. To-day I find her married to your son. I make the best of it—I forgive; you make the best of it—you forgive. Embrace us both—come, come. (*Both reject* RATTLETON.)

TWEEZ. If you *are* married, I suppose I *must* make the best of it ; but it's a terrible upset of a cherished plan. But I see Drudgley coming across the lawn.

RATTLE. Where—where? Dick, I've something particular to say to you in the next room. Come.

DICK. Something particular ?

RATTLE. (*Dragging him off.*) There's no time to be lost.
[*Exeunt,* R.

DRUDGLEY *enters at window—manner very formal*

DRUDG. Well, sir, I've come back, hoping to find you in a better frame of mind than when I had my last painful conversation with you.

TWEEZ. Painful conversation ? I didn't at all see that our conversation was at all *painful*—was it ?

DRUDG. It was to me—very painful. It was full of remarks prejudicial to a very honorable profession, of which I am but a humble member. We may be permitted to feel and to resent the indignities done to our class.

TWEEZ. I don't think you expected me to sign papers without reading them ?

DRUDG. Certainly not. I'm glad, however, to find your tone and language so much more moderate since we parted. Look over—scrutinize them—but remember you insulted me about business and about my wife, in a way that can only be excused by supposing that you were under the influence of—

TWEEZ. Drink—pray say, drink! I or you have been drinking this morning.

DRUDG. Allow me to observe that it is not I.

TWEEZ. Good, good—say it is I. Every one seems to be of the same opinion—there's only one sane person here, to all appearances.

DRUDG. And that is-

TWEEZ Mr. Rattleton.

DRUDG. He's here, is he? Well, I want him!

TWEEZ. On legal business?

DRUDG. Most of *my* business is legal—but now tell me—when shall we complete? when will you sign? The whole thing may fall through if not done directly.

TWEEZ. A little family affair has to be settled first, of which I was not aware this morning.

DRUDG. He evidently is suspicious. (*Aside.*) Where is Mr. Rattleton?

TWEEZ. Sit down—have something to eat. He'll be here directly.

DRUDG. Thank you. (*Sits down and begins luncheon.*)

Enter RATTLETON, R., *and goes up to* DRUDGLEY, L.

RATTLE. Ah! Mr. Drudgley, how are you? It is some time since we met. Have you any information touching that little matter?

DRUDG. (*Producing writ.*) Yes! I'll trouble you with this —excuse my serving it myself—I've never been able to lay my hand on you till now.

RATTLE. Now look here; you show me a writ, I'll show you a coin. (*Takes out the half-dollar.*) Look steadily at this; do you see anything peculiar about it.

DRUDG. (*Continuing to eat.*) No—it's only a half-dollar.

RATTLE. Look steadily. I pass my hands so—gaze on it —see—the spell works—he's mine—my second fluid to-day. [DRUDGLEY'S *fork has been arrested on its way to his mouth.*] There; he's quiet for a time.

TWEEZ. What's the matter?—is he choking?

Rattle. No; I've only electro-etceteraed him.

Tweez. What *do* you mean?

Rattle. Why, I've passed the fluid through his system and he becomes a portion of myself—loses his own individuality.

Tweez. Allow me to ask, have I been in an electro-etcetera state to-day?

Rattle. Something very like it.

Tweez. By way of rehearsal for your confounded soirée, I suppose?

Rattle. Unintentional—on my honor.

Tweez. And it is to you I am indebted for having forgiven my son and insulted my lawyer?

Rattle. Don't distress yourself—both are good actions. Look at me: I'll worm out his secrets. (*Takes* Drudgley's *hand*.) Tell me, man of parchment, what dost thou hope from me?

Drudg. You don't know, Mr. Rattleton—you've been running away from your best friend.

Rattle. Ah! you want to stick to me!

Drudg. If you knew all, you'd know that in my house is a document of the greatest importance to you.

Rattle. Not a second writ?

Drudg. No; the title deeds of an estate in Wisconsin—some five thousand dollars a-year.

Rattle. Wealth untold! Where is the innocent sheepskin?

Drudg. In box No. 7, right hand side, as you enter my office.

Rattle. Good. (*Makes passes.*)

Drudg. (*Puts the food in his mouth, and continues as before.*) So, as I was going to observe, Mr. Rattleton, you can't think how long I have looked for you.

Rattle. Not longer than I have for the title deeds of a little estate to Wisconsin, value about five thousand dollars a-year, now in box No. 7, on the right hand, as you enter your office

DRUDG. What! what!—who told you this? Believe me, Mr. Rattleton, I have sought you for *two* purporses—to recover a debt and to pay one—I shall be able to do both at the same time. I congratulate you heartily. Good morning.

RATTLE. No, no—hang me! I'll not part with you till I see the deeds safe in these hands of mine. I'll not trouble you again to look after me as you have done.

DICK *runs in,* R.

DICK. Father, father—here's Emily.

RATTLE. Stay—don't let her come in yet; it would be too much for me. Now, Mr. Drudgley, are you ready to start? —I want my deeds.

DRUDG. Come, come—

RATTLE. No delay, or I put my art once more in force against you. Here, Tweezer—here's your half-dollar. "Lie there, my art." (*Gives it.*) Dick, I congratulate you! Science has stood your friend, and mine—and yours, Tweezer. Drudgley, be honest; tell truth and shame the ancient gentleman, or beware my power; I've only got to do *so,* and *so.* (*Making passes.*) Ah! I forgot—I'd better do this in another place. (*To the Audience.*) Who'll lend me half-a-dollar?—I've five thousand a-year now. Don't speak all at once. Thank you, sir. If you will step up here with the coin, I shall no longer have to go about the world in want of A CONFEDERATE.

CURTAIN.

LODGINGS FOR SINGLE GENTLEMEN.

COLMAN THE YOUNGER.

WHO has e'er been in London, that overgrown place,
Has seen "Lodgings to Let" stare him full in the face,
Some are good and let dearly; while some, 'tis well known,
Are so dear, and so bad, they are best let alone.

Will Waddle, whose temper was studious and lonely,
Hired lodgings that took single gentlemen only;

But Will was so fat, he appear'd like a tun,
Or like two single gentlemen roll'd into one.

He enter'd his rooms, and to bed he retreated ;
But all the night long he felt fever'd and heated ;
And, though heavy to weigh as a score of fat sheep,
He was not, by any means, heavy to sleep.

Next night 'twas the same ! and the next ! and the next !
He perspired like an ox ; he was nervous and vex'd ;
Week passed after week, till by weekly succession,
His weakly condition was past all expression.

In six months his acquaintance began much to doubt him ;
For his skin, " like a lady's loose gown," hung about him.
He sent for a doctor, and cried, like a ninny,
" I have lost many pounds—make me well, there's a guinea."

The doctor look'd wise :--"A slow fever," he said ;
Prescribed sudorifices, and going to bed.
" Sudorifices in bed," exclaimed Will, " are humbugs !
I've enough of them there, without paying for drugs ! "

Will kick'd out the doctor :—but when ill indeed,
E'en dismissing the doctor don't always succeed ;
So, calling his host, he said, "Sir, do you know,
I'm the fat single gentleman, six months ago ?

" Look ye, landlord, I think," argued Will with a grin,
" That with honest intentions you first took me in :
But from the first night—and to say it I'm bold—
I've been so very hot, that I m sure I caught cold ! "

Quoth the landlord, " Till now, I ne'er had a dispute ;
I've let lodgings ten years,—I'm a baker to boot ;
In airing your sheets, sir, my wife is no sloven ;
And your bed is immediately—over my oven."

" The oven ! " says Will ;—says the host, " Why this passion ?
In that excellent bed died three people of fashion.

Why so crusty, good sir?"—"Zounds!" cried Will, in a taking
"Who wouldn't be crusty, with half a year's baking?"

Will paid for his rooms: cried the host, with a sneer,
" Well, I see you've been going away half a year."
" Friend, we can't well agree;—yet no quarrel," Will said
" But I'd rather not perish, while you make your bread."

THE FARMER AND THE COUNSELLOR.

SMITH

A counsel in the "Common Pleas,"
    Who was esteemed a mighty wit,
    Upon the strength of a chance hit,
Amid a thousand flippancies,
And his occasional bad jokes,
    In bullying, bantering, browbeating,
    Ridiculing and maltreating
Women, or other timid folks ;
In a late cause, resolved to hoax
A clownish Yorkshire farmer—one
    Who, by his uncouth look and gait,
    Appeared expressly meant by fate
For being quizzed and played upon.

So having tipped the wink to those
    In the back rows,
Who kept their laughter bottled down,
    Until our wag should draw the cork—
He smiled jocosely on the clown,
    And went to work.

" Well, Farmer Numskull, how go calves at York?
    " Why—not, sir, as they do wi' you;
    But on *four* legs instead of *two*."
" Officer," cried the legal elf,
Piqued at the laugh against himself,

"Do pray keep silence down below there!
Now look at me, clown, and attend,
Have I not seen you somewhere, friend?"
    "Yees, very like, I often go there."

"Our rustic's waggish—quite laconic,"
(The counsel cried, with grin sardonic,)
    "I wish I'd known this prodigy,
This genius of the clods, when I
    On circuit was at York residing.
Now, farmer, do for once speak true,
Mind, you're on oath, so tell me, you
Who doubtless think yourself so clever,
Are there as many fools as ever
    In the West Riding?"

"Why no, sir, no! we've got our share,
But not so many as when *you* were there."

THE PUGILISTS.

A STRIKING TALE.

ANONYMOUS.

Two boxers long enrolled by fame,
In *honors* such as bruisers claim,
Who having often sparred and fought,
And many a hardy victory bought,
By thumps, black eyes, and knock-down blows,
Eke broken head and bloody nose,
At length, like other heroes great,
That can control each humble state,
And keep the peaceful rogues in awe,
By what the vulgar call *club-law*,
Agreed, though friends, they should contest,
Which of themselves could fight the best,
Ambassadors went forth to treat,
Each Champion's council sage to greet;

Not with intent to offer peace,
And bid the sanguine passions cease;
No;—they the bruising art admired,
Were with the glorious contest fired:
Therefore they wider made the breach,
Conveyed in threats, from each to each.

At length these sage Ambassadors
Arranged all matters by the laws—
By *pugilistic laws* I mean,
Such as apply to fighting men;
For war, in every various scene,
Where blood and slaughter intervene,
Pays, or at least, appears to pay,
Respect to what it does away.
Thus, when a tyrant conq'ror seizes
Some state his fell ambition pleases,
He says they had infringed the *law*,
And holds them bound by right of war.
The Dutch, the Italians, and the Swiss,
Severely feel the truth of this.
Heaven guard our happy Isle! may we
From Conquerors' laws be ever free!

At length all matters are agreed,
The combatants, in form, proceed
To fam'd Olympus or Eleusis,
Whichever name the hearer chooses;
Yet think not they such ninnies prove,
Merely to fight for downright love;
No;—money, money is the prize,
To pay for bruises and black eyes.
The scientific gulls profound,
In close cabal are plac'd around.
Now hands they shake, and now set to,
To please the motley, mongrel crew.
A round is fought, and then another,
The odds run high on this and t'other;
Murmurs and shouts, and loud huzzas,

Sound forth each battered hero's praise;
But still, obedient to the laws,
'Twixt ev'ry round there is a pause.
"Time!" cries a voice—again they fight,
Besmear'd and bruis'd, a hideous sight!
Round after round with mix'd applause
Goes on, and "Time" ends every pause.

Time, call'd so oft, at length appears,
A goodly sage, thou worn in years;
At sight of him each savage started,
And, growling, would have thence departed:
Enchantment fixes them—they stand,
And trembling, view the glass in's hand;
While prostrate, panting on the ground,
The boxers by the spell are bound.
He speaks: "What would ye, knaves and fools,
Who thus disturb my peaceful rules?
Say, titled idlers, what have you
Among this motley group to do?
Within St. Stephen's echoing walls,
The Senate for your service calls;
Your country, too, demands your aid,
There let your prowess be display'd;
And let the foes of Britain know,
What to your native land you owe!—
For you, ye sots, that mingled round,
In murm'ring laziness are found—
Go to your several homes, and there
Let your starv'd offspring be your care;
Work—show your industry and love,
And thus to *Time* your value prove!
You, bleeding mastiffs, who have now
No power to urge the angry blow;
Yet whose hard hearts still burn with rage,
In the fierce conflict to engage:
On you is vainly spent my breath—
Behold, how near the victor—Death!
See ready his uplifted dart,

To pierce each bleeding bravo's heart."
This said—his garment opening wide,
Discover'd Death close at his side ;
Their fear he saw—the spell unbound,
And each prepar'd to quit the ground;
In haste, the late exulting crew,
Peers, boxers, mob and all withdrew.

HOW PAT SAVED HIS BACON.

ANONYMOUS.

EARLY one fine morning, as Terence O'Fleary was hard
at work in his potato-garden, he was accosted by his gossip,
Mick Casey, who he perceived had his Sunday clothes on.

"God's 'bud! Terry, man, what would you be afther
doing there wid them praties, an Phelim O'Loughlin's berrin'
goin' to take place? Come along, ma bochel! sure the
praties will wait."

"Och! no," sis Terry, "I must dig on this ridge for the
childer's breakfast, an' thin I'm goin' to confession to Father
O'Higgins, who holds a stashin beyont there at his own
house."

"Bother take the stashin!" sis Mick, "sure that 'ud wait
too." But Terence was not to be persuaded.

Away went Mick to the berrin'; and Terence, having finished "wid the praties," as he said, went down to Father
O'Higgins, where he was shown into the kitchen, to wait his
turn for confession. He had not been long standing there,
before the kitchen fire, when his attention was attracted by
a nice piece of bacon, which hung in the chimney-corner.
Terry looked at it again and again, and wished the childer
"had it at home wid the praties."

"Murther alive!" says he, "will I take it? Sure the
priest can spare it; an' it would be a rare thrate to Judy an'
the gossoons at home, to say nothin' iv myself, who hasn't
tasted the likes this many's the day." Terry looked at it

again, and then turned away, saying—" I won't take it— why would I, an' it not mine, but the priest's? an' I'd have the sin iv it, sure! I won't take it," replied he, " an' it's nothin' but the Ould Boy himself that's timptin' me! But sure it's no harm to feel it, any way," said he, taking it into his hand, and looking earnestly at it. " Och! it's a beauty; and why wouldn't I carry it home to Judy and the childer? An' sure it won't be a sin afther I confesses it!"

Well, into his great coat pocket he thrust it; and he had scarcely done so, when the maid came in and told him that it was his turn for confession.

" Murther alive! I'm kilt and ruin'd, horse and foot, now, joy, Terry; what'll I do in this quandary, at all, at all? By gannies! I must thry an' make the best of it, any how," says he to himself, and in he went.

He knelt to the priest, told his sins, and was about to receive absolution, when all at once he seemed to recollect himself, and cried out—

" Oh! stop—stop, Father O'Higgins, dear! for goodness' sake, stop! I have one great big sin to tell yit; only sir, I'm frightened to tell id, in the regard of never having done the like afore, sur, niver!"

" Come," said Father O'Higgins. " you must tell it to me."

" Why, then, your Riverince, I will tell id; but, sir, I'm ashamed like?"

" Oh, never mind! tell it," said the priest.

" Why, then, your Riverince, I went out one day to a gin-tleman's house, upon a little bit of business, an' he bein' in-gaged, I was showed into the kitchen to wait. Well, sur, there I saw a beautiful bit iv bacon hanging in the chimbly-corner. I looked at id, your Riverince, an' my teeth began to wather. I don't know how it was, sur, but I suppose the Divil timpted me, for I put it into my pocket; but, if you plaize, sur, I'll give it to you," and he put his hand into his pocket.

" Give it to me!" said Father O'Higgins; " no, certainly not; give it back to the owner of it."

"Why, then your Riverince, sur, I offered id to him, and he wouldn't take id."

"Oh! he wouldn't, wouldn't he?" said the priest; "then take it home, and eat it yourself, with your family."

"Thank your Riverince kindly!" says Terence, "an' I'll do that same immediately, plaize God; but first and foremost, I'll have the absolution, if you plaize, sir."

Terence received absolution, and went home rejoicing that he had·been able to save his soul and his bacon at the same time.

THE IRISH DRUMMER.

ANONYMOUS.

A SOLDIER, so at least the story goes,
   It was in Ireland I believe,
   Upon his back was sentenc'd to receive
Five hundred cat-o'-nine-tail blows;
Most sagely military law providing,
The *back* alone shall suffer for *backsliding*.
Whether his crime was great or small,
Or whether there was any crime at all,
   Are facts which this deponent never knew;
But though uncertain whether justly tried,
The man he knows was to the halbert tied,
   And hopes his readers will believe so too.
Suppose him, then, fast to the halberts bound,
His poor companions standing silent round,
   Anticipating ev'ry dreadful smack;
While Patrick Donovan, from Wicklow county,
Is just preparing to bestow his bounty,
   Or *beat quick time* upon his comrade's back.
Of stoics much we read in tales of yore,
   Of Zeno, Possidonious, Epictetus,
Who, unconcerned, the greatest torments bore,
   Or else these ancient stories strangely cheat us.
My hero was no stoic, it is plain:
   He could not suffer torments and be dumb,

But roared, before he felt the smallest pain,
  As though a rusty nail had pierc'd his thumb.
Not louder is the terror spreading note,
Which issues from the hungry lion's throat,
When o'er Numidian plains in search of prey,
He takes his cruel, his destroying way.
The first two strokes, which made my hero bleat,
Fell right across the confines of his seat,
On which he piteously began to cry,
  "Strike high! strike high! for mercy's sake strike high!"
Pat, of a mild, obliging disposition,
Could not refuse to grant his friend's petition;
An Irishman has got a tender heart,
And never likes to act a cruel part;
Pat gave a good example to beholders,
And the next stroke fell on his comrade's shoulders!
Our suffering hero now began to roar
As loud, if not much louder, than before;
At which Pat lost all patience, and exclaim'd,
While his Hibernian face with anger flam'd,
  "Perdition catch you!—can't your tongue be still?
There is no *plasing* you, strike where one will?"

MIKE HOOTER'S BEAR STORY.

HALL.

"IT's no use talkin'," said Mike, "'bout your Polar Bar, and you Grizly Bar, and all that sorter varmint what you read about. They ain't nowhar, for the big black customer that circumlocutes down in our neck o' woods, beats 'em all hollow. I've heard of some monsus explites kicked up by the brown bars, sich as totein' off a yoke o' oxen, and eatin' humans raw, and all that kind o' thing; and Capten Parry tells us a yarn 'bout a big white bar, what 'muses hisself climin' up the North Pole and slides down to keep his hide warm; but all that ain't a circumstance to what I've saw.

"You see," continued Mike, "there's no countin' on them varmints as I'se been usened to, for they comes as near bein' human critters as anything I ever see what doesn't talk. Why, if you was to hear anybody else tell 'bout the bar-fights I've had, you wouldn't b'leeve 'em, and if I wasn't a preacher, and could not lie none, I'd keep my fly-trap shot 'tell the day of judgment.

"I've heard folks say as how bars cannot think like other human critters, and that they does all the sly tricks what they does, from instink. Golly! what a lie! You tell me one of 'em don't know when you've got a gun, and when you ain't? Just wait a minit, an' my privit 'pinion is, when you've hearn me thro', you'll talk t'other side of your mouth.

"You see, one day, long time ago, 'fore britches come in fashion, I made a 'pointment with Ike Hamberlin, the steam doctor, to go out next Sunday to see whether we couldn't kill a bar, for you know bacon was skace, and so was money, and them fellows down in Mechanicsburg wouldn't sell on tick, so we had to 'pend on the varmints for a livin'.

"Speakin' of Mechanicsburg, the people down in that ar mud-hole ain't to be beat nowhere this side o' Christmas. I've hearn o' mean folks in my time, an' I've preached 'bout 'em a few; but ever sense that feller, Bonnel, sold me a pint of red-eye whiskey—an' half ov it backer juice—for a coon-skin, an' then guv me a brass picayune fur change, I've stopped talkin'. Why, that chap was closer than the bark on a hickory tree; an' ef I hadn't hearn Parson Dilly say so, I'd av swore it wasn't er fac, he was cotch one day steal-in' acorns from a blind hog. Did you ever hear how that hoss-fly died? Well, never mind. It was too bad to talk 'bout, but heap too good for him.

"But that ain't what I was spoutin' 'bout. As I was sayin' afore, we had to 'pend on the varmints fur a livin'. Well, Ike Hamberlin, you see, was always sorter jubious o' me, kase I kilt more bar nor he did; an', as I was sayin', I made a 'pointment with Ike to go out huntin'. Then, Ike, he thought he'd be kinder smart, and beat 'Old Preach' (as them Cole boys usen to call me), so, as soon as day crack, he hollered up his puppies, an' put! I spied what he was 'bout, for I hearn him laffin' to one o' his niggers 'bout it the night afore—so, I told my gal Sal to fill my private tickler full o' the old 'raw,' an' then fixed up an' tramped on arter him, but didn't take none o' my dogs. Ike hadn't got fur into the cane, 'fore the dogs they 'gan to whine an' turn up the har on ther backs ; an', bimeby, they all tucked tail, an' sorter sidled back to whar he was standin'. 'Sick him !' says Ike, but the critters wouldn't hunt a lick. I soon diskivered what was the matter, for I kalkilated them ours o' his'n wasn't worth shucks in a bar fight—so, I know'd thar was bar 'bout, if I didn't see no sine.

" Well, Ike he coaxed the dogs, an' the more he coaxed, the more they wouldn't go, an' when he found coaxin' wouldn't do, then he scolded and called 'em some of the hardest names ever you hearn, but the tarnation critters wouldn't budge a peg. When he found they wouldn't hunt no how he could fix it, he began cussin'. He didn't know I was thar. If he had er suspicioned it, he'd no more swore than he'd dar'd to kiss my Sal on er washin' day ; for you see both on us belonged to the same church, and Ike was class-leader. I thought I should er flummuxed! The dogs they sidled back, an' Ike he cussed ; an' I lay down an' rolled an' laughed sorter easy to myself, 'till I was so full I thort I should er bust my biler ! I never see ennything so funny in all my life ! There was I layin' down behind er log, fit to split, an' there was the dogs with their tails the wrong eend down, an' there was Ike a rarin' an' er pitchin'—er rippin' an' er tarin'—an' er cussin' wus nor a steamboat cap'n ! I tell you it fairly made my har' stan' on eend ! I never see er customer so riled afore in all my born days ! The dogs, they smelt bar sine, an' wouldn't budge a peg, an' arter Ike had a'most cussed the bark off'n a dog-wood saplin' by, he lent his old flint-lock rifle up agin it, and then he peeled off his old blanket an' laid her down,

too. I diskivered mischief was er cumin', fur I never see a
critter show rathy like he did. Torectly I see him walk
down to the creek bottom, 'bout fifty yards from where his
gun was, and then he 'gin pickin' up rocks an' slingin' um
at the dogs like bringer! Cracky! didn't he link it into
um? It minded me of David whalin' Goliah, it did! If
you'd er seed him, and hearn 'em holler, you'd er thought
he'd er knocked the nigh sites off'n every mother's son of
'em !

"But that ain't the fun yet. While Ike was er lammin'
the dogs, I hearn the alfiredest crackin' in the cane, an' I
looked up, an' thar was one of the eternalest whollopin'
bars cummin' crack, crack, through the cane an' kerslesh
over the creek, and stopped right plumb slap up whar Ike's
gun was. Torectly he tuck hold er the old shooter, an' I
thought I see him tinkerin' 'bout the lock, un' kinder whis-
lin', and blowin' into it. I was 'stonished, I tell you, but I
wanted to see Ike outdone so bad that I lay low and kep'
dark, an' in about a minit Ike got done lickin' the dogs, an'
went to git his gun. Jeemeny, criminy! if you'd only bin
whar I was! I do think Ike was the maddest man that
ever stuk an axe into a tree, for his har stuck right strait
up, and his eyes glared like two dog-wood blossoms! But
the bar didn't seem to care shucks for him, for he jist sot
the old rifle rite back agin the saplin', and walked on his
hind legs jist like any human. Then, you see, I gin to git
sorter jelus, and sez I to myself, 'Mister Bar,' sez I, 'the place
whar you's er stanin' ain't prezactly healthy, an' if you
don't wabble off from that purty soon, Missis Bar will be a
widder, by gum!' With that, Ike grabbed up old Missis
Rifle, and tuk most perticular aim at him, and, by hokey,
she snapped! 'Now,' sez I, 'Mister Bar, go it, or he'll make
bacon of you!' But the varmint didn't wink, but stood
still as a post, with the thumb of his right paw on the eend
of his smeller, and wiglin' his t'other finger, thus:—(*Mike
went through with the gyration.*) All this time, Ike, he stood
thar like a fool, er snappin' and er snappin', an' the bar, he

lookiﾑg kinder quare like, out er the corner o' his eye, an'
sorter laffin' at him. Torectly I see Ike take down the ole
shooter, and kinder kersamine the lock, an' when he done
that, he laid her on his shoulder, and shook his fist at the
bar, and walked toward home, an' the bar, he shuk his fist,
an' went into the canebrake, and then I cum off.'

Here all the Yazoo boys expressed great anxiety to know
the reason why Ike's gun didn't fire.

"Let's liker fust," said Mike, "an' if you don't caterpillar,
you can shoot me. Why you see," concluded he, "the long
and short of it is this, that the bar in our neck o' woods has
a little human in um, an' this feller know'd as much about
a gun as I do 'bout preachin', so when Ike was lickin' the
dogs, he jest blowed all the powder outen the pan, an' to
make all safe, he tuk the flint out too, and that's the way
he warn't skeered when Ike was snappin' at him."

THE CRITIC.

SARGENT.

ONCE on a time, the nightingale, whose singing
Had with her praises set the forest ringing,
Consented at a concert to appear :
Of course her friends all flocked to hear,
And with them many a critic, wide awake
To pick a flaw, or carp at a mistake.

She sang as only nightingales can sing ;
    And when she'd ended,
There was a general cry of "Bravo! splendid!"
    While she, poor thing,
Abashed and fluttering, to her nest retreated,
Quite terrified to be so warmly greeted.
The turkeys gobbled their delight ; the geese,
    Who had been known to hiss at many a trial,
    That this was perfect, ventured no denial :
It seemed as if the applause would never cease.

But 'mong the critics on the ground,
An ass was present, pompous and profound,
Who said,—" My friends, I'll not dispute the honor
That you would do our little prima donna :
Although her upper notes are very shrill,
And she defies all method in her trill,
She has some talent, and, upon the whole,
With study, may some cleverness attain.
Then, her friends tell me, she's a virtuous soul ;
But—but—"

      " But "—growled the lion, " by my mane,
I never knew an ass, who did not strain
To qualify a good thing with a but ! "
" Nay," said the goose, approaching with a strut,
" Don't interrupt him, sire ; pray let it pass ;
The ass is honest, if he is an ass ! "

" I was about," said Long Ear, " to remark,
That there is something lacking in her whistle ;
    Something magnetic,
    To waken cords and feelings sympathetic,
And kindle in the breast a spark
Like—like, for instance, a good juicy thistle."

The assembly tittered, but the fox, with gravity
    Said, at the lion winking,
" Our learned friend, with his accustomed suavity,
    Has given his opinion without shrinking ;
But, to do justice to the nightingale,
    He should inform us, as no doubt he will,
What sort of music 'tis, that does not fail
    His sensibilities to rouse and thrill."

" Why," said the critic, with a look potential,
    And pricking up his ears, delighted much
At Reynard's tone and manner deferential,—
    " Why, sir, there's nothing can so deeply touch
My feelings, and so carry *me* away,
    As a fine, mellow, ear-inspiring bray."

"I thought so," said the fox, without a pause ,
  "As far as you're concerned, your judgment's true.·
You do not like the nightingale, because
  The nightingale is not an ass like you!"

MR. CAUDLE WANTS A "LATCH-KEY."

JERROLD.

On my word, Mr. Caudle, I think it a waste of time to
come to bed at all now! The cocks will be crowing in a
minute. Keeping people up till past twelve. Oh yes!
you're thought a man of very fine feelings out of doors, I
dare say! It's a pity you haven't a little feeling for those
belonging to you at home. A nice hour to keep people out
of their beds! Why did I sit up, then? Because I chose
to sit up—but that's my thanks. No, it's no use your talking, Caudle; I never *will* let the girl sit up for you, and
there's an end. What do you say? Why does she sit up
with me, then? That's quite a different matter : you don't
suppose I'm going to sit up alone, do you? What do you
say? What's the use of *two* sitting up? That's my business. No, Caudle, it's no such thing. I *don't* sit up because
I may have the pleasure of talking about it; and you're an
ungrateful, unfeeling creature, to say so. I sit up because I
choose it; and if you don't come home all the night long—
and 'twill soon come to that, I've no doubt—still, I'll never
go to bed, so don't think it.

Oh, yes! the time runs away very pleasantly with you
men at your clubs—selfish creatures! You can laugh and
sing, and tell stories, and never think of the clock; never
think there's such a person as a wife belonging to you. It's
nothing to you that a poor woman's sitting up, and telling
the minutes, and seeing all sorts of things in the fire ; and
sometimes thinking that something dreadful has happened
to you; more fool she to care a straw about you! This is

all nothing. Oh, no! when a woman's once married, she's
a slave, worse than a slave, and must bear it all!

And what you men can find to talk about I can't think!
Instead of a man sitting every night at home with his wife,
and going to bed at a Christian hour, going to a club, to
meet a set of people who don't care a fig about him; it's
monstrous! What do you say? You only go once a week?
That's nothing at all to do with it; you might as well go
every night; and I dare say you will soon. But if you do,
you may get in as you can; I won't sit up for you, I can
tell you.

My health's being destroyed night after night, and—oh,
don't say it's only once a week; I tell you, that's nothing
to do with it—if you had any eyes, you would see how ill I
am; but you've no eyes for anybody belonging to you: oh,
no; your eyes are for people out of doors. It's very well
for you to call me a foolish, aggravating woman! I should
like to see the woman who'd sit up for you as I do. You
don't want me to sit up? Yes, yes, that's your thanks;
that's your gratitude; I'm to ruin my health, and to be
abused for it. Nice principles you've got at that club, Mr.
Caudle!

But there's one comfort—one great comfort; it can't last
long: I'm sinking; I feel it, though I never say anything
about it; but I know my own feelings, and I say it can't
last long. And then I should like to know who'll sit up for
you! Then I should like to know how your second wife—
what do you say? You'll never be troubled with another?
Troubled, indeed! I never troubled you, Caudle. No; it's
you who've troubled me; and you know it; though like a
foolish woman, I've borne it all, and never said a word about
it. But it *can't* last—that's one blessing.

Oh, if a woman could only know what she'd have to suffer, before she was married! Don't tell me you want to go
to sleep! If you want to go to sleep, you should come
home at proper hours! It's time to get up, for what I
know, now. Shouldn't wonder if you hear the milk in five

minutes—there's the sparrows up already; yes, I say the
sparrows; and, Caudle, you ought to blush to hear 'em.
No, Mr. Caudle: it *isn't* the wind whistling in the key-hole;
I'm not quite foolish, though you may think so. I know
wind from a sparrow!

Ha! when I think what a man you were before we were
married! But you're now another person, quite an altered
creature. But I suppose you're all alike; I dare say, every
poor woman's troubled and put upon, though I should hope
not so much as I am. Indeed, I should hope not! Going
and staying out, and—

What! You'll have a key? Will you? Not while I'm
alive, Mr. Caudle! I'm not going to bed with the door
upon the latch, for you or the best man breathing. You
won't have a latch; you'll have a Chubb's lock? Will you?
I'll have no Chubb here, I can tell you. What do you say?
You will have the lock put on to-morrow? Well, try it;
that's all I say, Caudle, try it. I won't let you put me in a
passion; but all I say is, try it.

A respectable thing, that, for a married man to carry
about with him—a street-door-key! That tells a tale, I
think. A nice thing for the father of a family! A key!
What! to let yourself in and out when you please! To
come in, like a thief in the middle of the night, instead of
knocking at the door like a decent person! Oh, don't tell
me that you only want to prevent my sitting up. If I
choose to sit up, what's that to you? Some wives indeed,
would make a noise about sitting up, but you've no reason
to complain, goodness knows!

Well, upon my word, I've lived to hear something. Carry
the street-door key about with you! I've heard of such
things with young good-for-nothing bachelors, with nobody
to care what became of 'em; but for a married man to leave
his wife and children in a house with the door upon the
latch—don't talk to me about the Chubb—a great deal you
must care for us. Yes, it's very well for you to say, that you
only want the key for peace and quietness—what's it to you,

if I like to sit up? You've no business to complain; it can't distress you. Now, it's no use your talking; all I say is this, Caudle; if you send a man to put on any lock here, I'll call in a policeman; as I'm your married wife, I will.

No, I think when a man comes to have the street-door key, the sooner he turns bachelor again the better. I'm sure Caudle, I don't want to be any clog upon you. Now, it's no use your telling me to hold my tongue, for I—What? I give you the headache, do I? No, I don't, Caudle; it's your club that gives you the headache; its your smoke, and your—well! if ever I knew such a man in all my life! there's no saying a word to you! You go out, and treat yourself like an emperor, and come home at twelve at night, or any hour, for what I know, and then you threaten to have a key, and—and—and—

"I *did* get to sleep at last," says Caudle, " amid the falling sentences of 'take children into a lodging'—'separate maintenance'—' won't be made a slave of '—and so forth."

HUMBUGGING A TOURIST.

PAULDING.

Characters.

PHIL. PETERS, *a New Yorker, personating* MR. BRAGG *from Vicksburg.*

SAM. MARKHAM, *a Philadelphian.*

HUSKISSON HODGSON, *a Brummagem Beau and a Tourist.*

PHIL. Tell me who is this pompous signor, swelling and strutting through the street. By his port and majesty, I should judge him to be the British Lion.

SAM. Ay, that's his figure looming up the street. Shall we call him in as he comes this way, and bait the bull?

PHIL. By all manner of means.

SAM. Well, first let me give you a hint or too. I have told you what he is—he has forced his way into good society, nobody can tell how—can see nothing admirable in this country or its institutions, of course—but is eloquent on oysters. And now, Phil, you must play the "half-horse, half-alligator," for the nonce. Mind you give it to him in strong doses, and fear not overacting your part; for the poor simpleton has such extraordinary notions of the Western country, that he will swallow anything, however preposterous; and it is a pity he should be disabused, he is so innocent in his belief. (*Knocks at the window.*) Ho, Hodgson, come in, and have a chat with us. (*Turning to* PHIL.) You are now Mr. Bragg, and lo! the victim comes. (*Enter* HODGSON.) Mr. Hodgson, how are you, this morning? Allow me to introduce my friend, Mr. Bragg, of Vicksburg. (PHIL *turns away, with his hands in his pockets, and whistles "Old Dan Tucker." Aside to* HODGSON.) He is, I assure you, a very pleasant fellow—an excellent specimen of the frank Western man—and will be delighted to give you any information respecting the country, habits of the people, and so on.

HODGSON. (*In a cautious whisper.*) But are you sure he is not dangerous? Has he no Bowie-knives, pistols, or anything of the kind about him?

SAM. (*In the same tone.*) Well—not more then the usual allowance—a "Planter's Protector," or so, perhaps or a sword-cane—nothing more. But how were you pleased, last night, at Mrs. Nogood's?

HODG. Oh—Miss Garafeliaw was pausitively divoine; she hung upon my aurm, and while I entertained her with the description of my ancestral halls—

SAM. (*Aside.*) Conceited ass!

PHIL. (*Aside.*) Pheugh! ancestral halls! his paternal cotton mills. Heaven save the mark!

HODG. The words of love and mutual affection rising to our lips—

PHIL. (*Aside hurriedly.*) I must stop this, or Sam will be frantic. (*Walking quickly to the window.*)

SAM. Why, Phil—(excuse me, Mr. Bragg, for being so familiar)—what on earth is the row?

HODG. (*Aside.*) What is—auh—the savage going to do now?

PHIL. Why, may my boiler be eternally busted, if there isn't that are young lady I was keepin' company with yesterday, a travelling along with another feller. But I'll be down upon him like an Arkansaw flood—I'll be into him like a Mississippi sawyer. Where are my pistols? Whoo-oo-oo-oop!

HODG. Oh, Mr. Bragg, for Heaven's sake! in the name of mercy, don't, don't!

SAM. Oh pshaw, Bragg, for our sakes now, stay and take a quiet julep, and defer your performances till afterwards.

PHIL. Waal, I suppose I mought as well, specially as I reckon he ain't of no account, any how. I *will* if you'll give us a chaw tobacca.

SAM. (*Rings the bell*—WAITER *comes.*) John, go across the way, and bring us some juleps, and a paper of tobacco. Don't stand there staring at me, but go—quick—fly—and be back in a theatrical minute.

PHIL. (*To* SERVANT.) Mind—pigtail! [*Exit* SERVANT.

HODG. (*Aside to* SAM.) But don't you think!—(*He draws his hand across his throat.*)

SAM. (*In a whisper to* HODG.) Oh, no. I assure you we are perfectly safe; he does not mean anything by it. (*Juleps are brought; each helps himself.* SAM *beckons to his* SERVANT *and whispers.*) Now, John, whatever I order you to do when that stout gentleman is here, do it as if it were the commonest thing in the world. You understand me!

JOHN. (*Grinning.*) Yes, sir!   [*Exit* JOHN.

HODG. (*Sipping julep.*) By Gemini, that's good. Are you aware, gents, that this is the finest thing in your country? People talk about you rivers, and all that sort of thing, and they call cotton your staple production, but for my pawt, I consider your juleps and your oysters to be the only things worthy of imitation. Fact is, 'pon honor, I have some idea of taking a few oysters out to improve the breed in England. Oyster, gents, I may say—oysters are the only things which redeem your country.

PHIL. Do you mean, Mr. What's-your-name, to insinuate that this here country, called the United States of Ameriky, requires anything to redeem its character, or any thing else? If you do, may be I won't be into your eyes in less then no time, like a real Kaintucky poker a-rooting in the woods

HODG. (*Covering his eyes with his hands.*) Oh, no, no no!

PHIL. Oh, waal, if you didn't mean nothin', Socrates Bragg is not the man to take offence at a trifle; and I reckon, besides, you ain't no great shakes.

HODG. (*Aside.*) "No great shakes"! I must inquiawr if he means to insult me. (*Aloud.*) But Mr. Markham, I see no spit-boxes about your parlor here—auh—as I have been led to expect!

SAM. Oh, we have given them up, and expectorate in the French style into our pocket-handkerchiefs—those, at least, who have enjoyed the advantages of travelling in Europe.

HODG. Indeed! (*Aside to* SAM.) I would like to ask him (*Pointing to* PHIL) about Bowie-knives and such things.

SAM. (*Aside to* HODG.) Well, do it. These Western fellows like to talk big.

HODG. (*Turning to* PHIL.) May I inquiawr, Mr. Bragg, whethaw Bowie-knives are as common now in Cincinnati and the other frontier towns as they used to be?

PHIL. *May you inquire?* Do you mean to insult me, Mr. Hodgkins? Are we not among gentlemen here? Ain't we all plain spoken?

HODG. I mean no offence, 'pon honor.

PHIL. 'Nuff said. Waal, as to Bowie-knives, sir, they're going out—

HODG. (*Piously.*) Thank Heaven!

PHIL. (*Pretending not to notice his exclamation.*) And now, most use Bolen's six-barrelled revolving, self-cocking pistols, with a small sprinkle of a Bowie-knife on the end of them, in case of emergency; though some prefer Colt's repeaters just for the sake, I calculate, of being singular and uncommonlike.

HODG. Good Lord, have mercy upon us ! What a state of society ! But are these weapons publicly carried ?

PHIL. Oh, yes. We occasionally practise in the streets ; and if a little boy, or a stranger is once in a while found dead, why it's nobody's business, and the coroner's inquest brings in a verdict of " accidental death."

HODG. The infernal spirit of democracy ! Heaven defend me from such a country. But are rifles still in common use ?

PHIL. Rifles? Why, what else should we use ?

HODG. Auh—I thought perhaps there might be a market there for double-barrelled guns; and—auh—indeed, that is pawt—auh—of my business out here—to dispose of. Hum —hum—(*Aside.*) By Gemini, I came within an ace letting the cat out of the bag.

PHIL. Mr. Hodg—podge—

HODG. (*Interrupting him.*) Hodgson, sir, if you please.

PHIL. Mr. Hodgson, then, take my advice, and, if you hope to escape with anything left of you, speak not in our Western country of a double-barrelled gun. We don't tolerate 'em, sir.

HODG. Is it pawsible ?

PHIL. Yes, sir ; I ventured once to purchase one out of curiosity, and the excitement against it, sir, was so intense in my neighborhood, that I had to throw it into the Mississippi. I tried the infernal big-mouthed cretur once, and may I be eternally split up into firewood, sir, if the shot didn't come out just like a fog, and when it disappeared, all that I could find of my bird was the end of his bill. No, sir, the rifle is our weapon ; with that we can shoot anything' from buffalo down to an Englishman, or a sandpiper.

HODG. (*Aside.*) How he makes one shiver ! Sandpipers with rifles ! Good Heavens ! the extravagance of these Western people is really awful. No wonder they are obliged to repudiate ; and there, by the way, is a hint for my book.

(Aloud.) But, Mr. Bragg, is tarring and feathering common?

PHIL. Law bless you, yes! Why I myself was tarred and feathered once, and just becoss my bank bust up, and I could not pay my creditors.

SAM. *(Aside.)* That's right, Phil; smite him on the hip, and spare not.

HODG. *(In agitation.)* What a land! what a land! But, Mr. Bragg, were you ever blown up?

PHIL. Blown up, sir! Warn't I raised on the Mississippi, and lived on steam since I was a babby? Why, you might as well ask me if I've been weaned. It's the commonest thing in natur. Blown up?—more times than I can count up, sir?

HODG. What, Mr. Bragg, were your sensations?

PHIL. Why, sir, it is the pleasantest and most elevating feeling you can imagine. May I be scalped, sir, if it is not just like being kicked into chaos. No man, sir, knows what the sublimity of life is until he has had a biler bust under him. You may take my word for that, sir. And now, good morning, gentleman. (PHIL *rises to depart.*) But before I go, I will tell you, sir *(turns to* HODG.*)*, a true and interesting story—if it isn't, may I be—well—about a burst up.

Waal, sir, I was going up stream, one day, to St. Louis, and I had a horse on board—(a finer horse, by the way, sir, never trod turf. His name was Roanoke—my ancestors come from the Old Dominion, sir), and I sees that something was the matter with him, and a knowing hoss he was to smell out mischief. So I goes up, and says I, "Roanoke, what snag ha' you run against now? Do you want some feed, old boy?" says I.

He shook his head.

"Are you cold?" says I.

He shook his head.

"Is the biler going to bust?" says I.

He nods his head.

"Right straight?" says I.

He nods his head again.

I unties the halter as fast as I can, and I sings out "Gentlemen, I'll bet ten to one this boat's biler busts before sunset." "Done," and "done," shouts a dozen, when *bang* goes *both* bilers like a clap of thunder run mad. May I be scalped, sir, if I and my horse weren't the only creatures that escaped. So I lost all my bets, and was obliged to resolve myself into a committee, sir, in a cypress swamp, to exonerate the captain, engineer, hands, and biler from all blame, collectively and individually. I tell you what, sir, may I never taste Monongahela again, if I didn't get aboard the next up boat in a mighty thick rile. *Good morning*, gentlemen!

SAM. (*Winks to* PHIL.) Don't go yet, Bragg, sit down again, now, and tell us a little more about your parts. Mr. Hodgson is very much interested in that section of the country, and a stranger—

PHIL. Oh, waal, I'm always ready cocked to go off for a *stranger's* information.

HODG. Thank you—auh—what sort of people have you out there?

PHIL. Waal, we've got some a'most all kinds: Pukes, Wolverines, Snags, Hoosiers, Griddle-greasers, Buckeyes, Corn-crackers, Pot-soppers, Hard-heads, Hawkeyes, Rackensacks, Linsey-woolseys, Red-horses, Mud-heads, Greenhorns, Canada-patriots, Loafers, Masons, Anti-masons, Mormons, and some few from the Jerseys, and other outside places of creation.

HODG. Heavens! All savage tribes, I presume; but I thought your government—auh—had removed all the Indians beyond the Mississippi.

PHIL. No, sir; there are still many savages this side the river.

HODG. What is the average product of your lands, per acre, Mr. Bragg, in a good season?

PHIL. Oh—of snakes, ten cords is considered a very fair yield, making two bushels of rattles, or more when threshed out; but that's according to the age of the reptiles—of mosquitoes, four bushels—of other vermin, six bushels is called a tolerable crop.

HODG. Good Lord! Snakes by the cord! But I mean corn and other grain.

PHIL. *Stranger*, in the West we never keep account of sich things. We save enough to eat, and feed our hogs, and send the rest to market; and if the rivers ain't dry, and the steamboats don't get snagged, run into, blown up, or seized by the sheriff, it gets there in the course of time and we presume is sold; for that's the last we hear of it.

HODG. And you have no agents to attend to it when it arrives?

PHIL. Oh—yes—we hires agents o' course.

HODG. And you never call on them to give account of their sales and receipts?

PHIL. No, *sir*, no—it would be as much as a man's life is worth to do so unpopular a thing. It's an unheard of notion, *stranger*—an obsolete idea. Nobody thinks of such a thing, except once in a while a mean feller, and he has to cut stick—quit our parts, sir, in short order, I reckon. Tramp's the word, and he emigrates, sir. 'Sides, there's the chance o' your agent's drawin' on you."

HODG. Drawing on you? With funds of yours in his hands, auh?

PHIL. Yes, sir—click! And may be you find half an ounce o' lead lodged in your phrenological developments.

HODG. Shocking!

PHIL. Waal, jist to show you the workin' of the thing: you see we made Bill Toddy our agent—good fellow—fust rate chap—great on liquor. Now supposin' I goes to New Orleans, and says I to Bill, "Look here, young 'un, jist fork over that are change, will you?" What do you think Bill does?

HODG. Why, he takes out his ledger, balances his account, and pays you what he owes on your sales.

PHIL. That jist shows how much you know of human

natur, Mr. Hodgeskin. Now I should calkerlate that Bill
would naterally get his back up at that, and say—" Soo
Bragg, you're a poor devil "—or, " Soc Bragg, you're a
durned dropsical water-drinker "—or, " Soc Bragg, you're
everlastingly beneath my notice." And then, we'd have
one of the awfulest musses that ever did take place in New
Orleans.

HODG. Mr. Bragg, the state of society in your country is
even more disorganized than I had supposed.

PHIL. Yes, sir-r-r, it can't be beat, as you say. Most
people in furrin parts have every kind of amphibious ideas
of our diggins. You don't know what a glorious place it is
out West. It is of an entire different stripe from foggy
England, where you have to drink port, and ale, and beer,
and sich like onnateral tipple. It's another kind of streak,
sir-r-r.

HODG. Auh—Mr. Bragg—auh—do you drink much malt
liquor in your pawts? auh—I have a brothow—auh—that
is—yes—yaas—

PHIL. Look here, *stranger*, why don't you speak as if you
warn't afraid o' what you were sayin' instead of coughin'
like an old steamboat—puff—auh—puff—auh? Speak out
like a ringed pig.

HODG. I merely ausked if you drank much malt liquor in
your pawts.

PHIL. Do we drink spring water? No sir! we drink
Tom and Jerry some—gin-cocktails putty considerably—
but mostly stone fence bare-footed!

HODG. Eh! what! bare-footed! I had no idea, I must
confess, of the misery of this country. Dear me, I'll write
a communication, when I get home, to some of the charit-
able societies. No shoes!—not even moccasins! (*Aside.*) It's
a judgment on them for their oppression of their colored
brethren.

PHIL. No shoes? What does the man mean, Mr. Markham?

SAM. I fancy Mr. Hodgson doesn't take your meaning.

PHIL. That's it, eh ? I was afaid the *stranger* was pokin' fun at me—and then I'm dangerous.

HODG. Oh, no, no, no ! I assure you.

PHIL. Well, stranger, whar *was* you raised ? I thought even a Yankee knew that " stone fence bare-footed " is the polite English for whiskey uncontaminated—pure, sir.

HODG. (*Aside.*) What—auh—a frightful patois they speak.

PHIL. (*Aside to* SAM.) Keep him on that track, Sam, and I'll astonish him.

SAM. I believe, however, Mr. Bragg, that some parts of the country are very poor indeed.

PHIL. Poor, sir ! It's considerably the richest country that ever was created. Why, I've seen many a tree it took a man and a boy to look to the top of.

HODG. That's a very singular circumstance.

PHIL. Fact, sir.

SAM. But I mean, Mr. Bragg, that meat is sometimes very scarce.

PHIL. Oh, *meat !*—yes. I was out one year in a log cabin, a little out of the common trail, and sometimes we didn't see a piece of meat for three months at a time, and lived perty much on sweet punkins.

HODG. Punkins ! Good Heavens ! This goes beyond anything I ever heard or read of before. They may talk about famine in India, and poverty in Ireland, but never can there be greater misery than this. But did you not become very weak under such a diet, Mr. Bragg ?

PHIL. Waal, sir, we fell off some, but were pretty nigh as strong as a ten-horse steam ingyne for all that. Why, stranger, my father that spring swum across the Big Satan, in a freshet, with a dead painter in his mouth, and a live alligator full splurge after him. It was a tight race, I tell you, and I *did* laugh, and no mistake, to see the old man puttin' out. The crittur just bit off the heel of his boot as he got ashore. *He did !*

HODG. Horrible ! A dead painter between his teeth ! And how did he come by this untimely end ?

PHIL. What, the painter? how should he? My father shot him, sir, and a most almighty good shot it was, or *I'm* no judge. He took him sitting, sir, but—

HODG. (*Trembling.*) And—and—what was the provocation, sir?

PHIL. Why, I rayther allow the animal was just takin' a sketch of him, and would have had him, sir.

HODG. Good Heavens! Shoot a gentleman—an innocent, unoffending artist—

PHIL. Shoot a what? I'm speakin' of a painter, sir.

HODG. And isn't a painter a fellow-Christian—a man as well as you? hasn't he a soul to be saved?

PHIL. Well, that ar' beats—a painter a Christian! Why, sir, we consider them in our parts the worst kind o' heathen!

SAM. (*Stifling a laugh.*) I apprehend, Mr. Bragg, that Mr. Hodgson lies under an error; he thinks you mean a man that paints—signs, you know, and portraits.

PHIL. No, now? does he? Well, I'm dirned if he ain't a greenhorn! Why, mister, a painter's a wild animal—a catamount, sir—an exaggerated kind o' Bengal tiger!

SAM. I fancy, too, that Mr. Hodgson misapprehends your account of the lack of meat. I dare say you had plenty of venison.

PHIL. Oh, yes—plenty of venison—no lack of vittels.

HODG. Venison!

SAM. And wild turkeys, perhaps?

PHIL. Wild turkeys! oh, yes—all out doors are full of them; 'sides 'coons, squirrels, beavers' tails, 'chucks, bear-meat, skunks, and other varmints. Lots of *fodder* we had, that *are* a fact—but no *meat!* Tell you what, sir, it's paddling right up the stream in a canoe, to live without meat. The old man did grumble some, I tell you!

HODG. What *does* the man mean?—Wild turkeys and venison—and no meat?

SAM. I believe I must explain for you, Mr. Hodgson. The term *meat* in the West is understood to apply solely to *salt pork.*

HODG (*Aside.*) What a monstrous slang these savages speak! It's impossible to understand it. (*Aloud.*) Have you any Englishmen out there?

PHIL. Britishers?—I tell you, sir, we have the scum of all creation in our parts.

HODG. Auh, auh! auh—auh—what is the usual currency of that part of the country? Auh—what do you pay your debts with?

PHIL. Ha! ha! ha! (*Laughs.*) Pay our debts with?—that's a good joke—may be I won't tell that when I get home. We *slope*, sir, absquatulate!

HODG. (*To* SAM.) What does he mean?

SAM. (*To* HODG.) Hush!—don't press him on that point—it's dangerous!

PHIL. As for our currency, it's rayther promiscuous, as I may say, jest now—mostly 'coon skins, howsomever. You see the Owl Creek, and the Wild Cat, and Sore Bear, and the Salt River, and the Alligator banks all went slam bang to eternal smash, and since then, it's ben very *mixed*.

SAM. Didn't a certain bank, called the Big Riley Bubble, explode also?

PHIL. Take care, Mr. Markham, I don't stand that, sir-r-r —I have a mighty pisen feelin' about that concern.

HODG. Why, Mr. Bragg, had you any interest—

PHIL. *Stranger*, if you don't shet your mouth a little closer than a Gulf clam, I'll fix your flint in short order.

HODG. Excuse me, Mr. er-Bragg; didn't mean to offend, 'pon honor.

PHIL. Sir-r-r, *I* was President of the Big Riley Bubble Bank. *I* was rode on a sharp rail—and if you allude to it again, may I be eternally condemned to be fireman to the slowest boat in *all* creation, if I don't scalp you in several seconds less than no time. We can *do* that, sir, whar I was raised.

HODG. I'm dumb—auh!

SAM. Lethe shall be with me another name for the Big Riley.

Hodg. Have you any knowledge of the State of Arkansas, Mr. Bragg?

Phil. I've *ben* thar, I reckon—I *have* hunted all over them parts, almost clean out to the jumping off place of creation.

Hodg. Auh—auh—do you know anything of Ramdown County? Ah, auh—my fauther took some lands there for a debt about ten years ago, and I have some idea of—of going out there to examine the property. There are several flourishing villages upon it, as I perceive by the map I have of it.

Phil. Do I know Ramdown County? I'd like to see the man would tell me I don't, that's all. I'm getting tired of a peaceful life. It makes me bilious!—(Hodg. *edges away from him.*) Ramdown County, sir, is an eternal bog—one of the ugliest, dirtiest, deepest, nastiest, cussedest swamps that ever was created. (*Solemnly.*) Mr. Hodgkins, you had better venture into New Orleans in yeller fever time than show your face there. Why, sir, the only dry locations in it are taken up by the wust kind o' squatters—and if you escape, sir, the alligators, rattlesnakes, moccasins, bears, painters, quagmires, hurricanes, highwaymen, freshets, Inguns, and bilious fevers, you will be murdered by the settlers, and *no* mistake!

Sam. (*Aside to* Phil.) Phil, that is too bad!

Hodg. What a dreadful picture! But the towns—Oxford, Babylon, Sodom, Nineveh, Moscow?

Phil. *Towns*, sir! There isn't but one log cabin in the lot —at Sodom, sir—and that's a place even the boatmen didn't like to stop at. (*In a solemn whisper.*) It's a mortal *unhealthy* place for strangers—several have *disappeared* there?

Hodg. Dear! dear! dear! catch me there! But Moscow and the others?

Phil. Moscow is fifty feet above ordinary water mark, and only accessible in wet seasons—and has no inhabitants. Oxford is fifteen feet under water at all times, and death for fever and ague, besides being dreadfully infested with mosquitoes, alligators, and howling savages. Babylon was swallowed up some years ago by an earthquake; and Nineveh was washed away by the Red River last spring, *and* it deserved to be swept off, sir, for I am credibly informed, there was nothing to drink in the place. What's the use of such poor places, but to be washed away? Any more inquiries, *stranger?* happy to give you information.

HODG. No, I thank you, sir—auh—I believe I won't go there.

PHIL. *Stranger,* I wouldn't. It's a powerful sickly country for people who ask too many questions, and ain't satisfied with what they get there—it goes against one's grain when we see a man *stuck up,* I tell you, and we let him know it quick. And now I'll cut dirt!

HODG. (*Producing a note book.*) Allow me one—auh—moment, Mr. Bragg—Have you any objection to my taking a note of this conversation for a—auh—a work I have in contemplation?

SAM. (*Aside.*) He bites, by all that is incredible.

PHIL. Why—Mr. Hodgson, it doesn't strike me as exactly the thing to take down a man's words in this way, but if you particularly desire it, durn me if I can refuse such a trifle.

HODG. I should, sir—auh—esteem it as a particular favaw.

PHIL. Then, sir, you have my permission. Good morning, again. (*Aside to* SAM, *who follows him to the door.*) Didn't I throw a pretty good broadside into the Cockney?

SAM. Faith, you gave it to him like Stephen Decatur. And what do you think of the beast?

PHIL. That you may safely warrant him at any cattle show as a genuine imported bull.   [*Exit* PHIL.

HODG. (*Aside, writing in his note book.*) All the Americans are shockingly profane. (*Rising to take his leave.*) An extraordinary man that, Mr. Markham.

SAM. Very, in his way. There are many such beyond the mountains.

HODG. Well—auh—Mr. Markham, good day. I must go and commit this conversation to writing. [*Exit* HODGSON.

SAM. There goes the model of a Cockney tourist in America.   [*Exit* SAM.

THE WIDOW'S VICTIM.

AN ETHIOPIAN INTERLUDE.

Characters.

JENNY—TOMMY—JOHNNY.

(*For Complete Stage Directions see page* 64.)

Enter JENNY, C.

JENNY. There now, my missus is gone out, the cook is busy, and the laundress is ironing, and I, Jenny the chambermaid, having finished my day's work, can employ my time as I please; and, as the old saying is, "When the cat's away the mice will play."

I was to the theatre last night with my Tommy; he belongs to one of those Dramatic Associations, and he acts; he says he's going to make an actress of me. My missus is greatly troubled by a countryman hangin' around here, and so she told me to send for my Tommy, to dress himself up and frighten the countryman away. I sent for him some time go, and I wonder what keeps him so long?

TOMMY. (*Outside*, C., *stumbles.*) Curse that pail!

JENNY. (L. H. C.) That's his voice. This way, Tommy!

TOMMY. (*Outside*, C.) Lead me, lead me, ye virgins, to that kind voice. (*Enters*, C., *and embraces her.*) Camille!

JENNY. Armand!

TOMMY. Camille! Camille! Camille!

JENNY. (*Throws him off.*) Armand, I've sworn to hate, to despise you; but no, no! I cannot! (*They embrace and walk to* C.)

TOMMY. Angels were painted fair to look like thee. Confound it, I've almost broke my shin stumbling over that pail.

Why is it, Jenny, you will leave pails standing around for people to fall over; but—

    My love, my life, my Violante,

    Have you got anything nice to eat in the pantry!

JENNY. I've got some co-l-d goo-se.

TOMMY. Aha! ill-omened bird! name it not, or I shall go into *hiss-terics ;* but what did you send for me for?

JENNY. Oh! I almost forgot, I'm so stage-struck. There's a countryman coming around here, bothering my mistress a great deal, and she can't get rid of him; so she wants you to frighten him away.

TOMMY. Oh! she wants me to get up a little play to frighten him away, does she?

JENNY. Yes.

TOMMY. I'm the very boy to do it; don't you remember how nicely I played Claude Melnotte last Thursday night?

JENNY. Yes; and how I wished I had been Pauline, for I know every word of the part!

TOMMY. You do!

JENNY. Yes, sir, I do.

TOMMY. Then suppose while we're waiting for this old countryman we have a little bit of it.

JENNY. All right!

TOMMY. Do you recollect the last part of the third act?

JENNY. Yes.

TOMMY. All right ; get your posish. (*Jenny goes to* L. H. C. *and fixes dress.*) What are you doing that for?

JENNY. That's my trail.

TOMMY. Oh! Are you ready?

JENNY. Yes.

TOMMY. Then go it.

JENNY. (*Imitating some actress.*) Claude, take me; thou canst not give me wealth, station, titles, but thou canst give me a true and loving heart I will work for thee, toil for thee, bear with thee ; and never, never shall these lips reproach thee for the past. (*They embrace.*) How's that, Tommy?

TOMMY. That's bully; that's a great deal better than Miss Fish done it the last time we saw her.

JENNY. You don't mean Miss Fish, Tommy; you mean Miss Heron.

TOMMY. Miss Heron! well ain't herrin' fish? of course they are—Yankee sardines. Now then, Jenny, it's my turn. Are you ready?

JENNY. Yes.

TOMMY. Then look out. This is the heaviest blow of all—

JENNY. What blow?

TOMMY. Why what you've jest bin blowin' about. What a heart I've wronged! Farewell, mother; I'll see thee again a better man than a prince. And thou—thou so fondly loved, so guiltily betrayed, all is not yet lost; for if I live, the name of him thou hast once loved shall not rest dishonored; but if I fall midst the roar and carnage of battle, my soul shall fly back to thee; more—more would I speak to thee: to bless, to pray—but no, no; farewell, farewell, farewell.

As TOMMY *is going off* C., JOHNNY *enters and* TOMMY *treads on his toe.*

JOHNNY. Oh! oh! right on my favorite corn!

TOMMY. Peace, old man, I have a prior claim!

JOHNNY. I didn't know that, sir.

TOMMY. I outbid you, sordid huckster, for this priceless jewel. There! there's the sum twice told; blush not to take it. (*Throws purse.*)

JOHNNY. Nary a blush. (*Puts purse in pocket.*)

TOMMY. There's not a coin but which has been bought in a nation's cause and with a soldier's blood.

JENNY. Ah! that voice! it is—it is—

TOMMY. Thy husband. (*They embrace.*)

JOHNNY. I've made a mistake, and got into a lunatic asylum. (*Pulls out stocking for a handkerchief.*)

JENNY. (*Aside to* TOMMY.) That's him.

TOMMY. Is it? what's the matter?

JENNY. He's like Othello when Iago's been stuffin' him up. I'll frighten him.

TOMMY. Go it.

JENNY. H-u-s-h—sh ! the handkerchief—the handkerchief. (*Snatches stocking from* JOHNNY.)—the handkerchief ! (*Goes off* R. H.)

JOHNNY. Here, young woman, you've got my handker. fitch !

TOMMY. (*Pulls* JOHNNY *to* C.) Come here. Were you ever on the stage ?

JOHNNY. Yes, I drove on de Knickerbocker once.

TOMMY. No, no ! I mean the stage Shakespeare speaks of as holding the mirror up to nature.

JOHNNY. Yes ; I've got one in my room seven by nine.

TOMMY. No, no ! I mean the same kind of a stage as you will find in a theatre.

JOHNNY. Oh ! like the play actors have.

TOMMY. Yes. What kind of a voice have you got for tragedy ?

JOHNNY. Oh, I've got scrougin' ole voice fur tragedy.

TOMMY. Well, supposing I should step up to you, slap you on the shoulder, and call you a villain and a traitor to the State, what reply would you make ?

JOHNNY. I should say that was very ungentlemanly language.

TOMMY. No, no ! you should say—Liar ! Now get over on that side   Are you ready ?

JOHNNY. Yes, sir.

TOMMY. (*Slapping him on the back.*) Thou art a villain and a traitor to the State.

JOHNNY. (*Very low.*) Liar !

TOMMY. Oh ! that is the weakest lie I ever did hear ; come over here and call me a villain.

JOHNNY. You're a willain and a traitor to de State.

TOMMY. L-i-a-r !

JOHNNY. (R. H. C. *frightened.*) I didn't mean it.

TOMMY. That's the way I wanted you to speak to me.

Come here. (*Goes to* c.) Did you ever see any plays performed?

JOHNNY. Yes, sir.

TOMMY. What were they?

JOHNNY. Macbeth, Toodles, and all dem fellers.

TOMMY. What do you think you could play in Macbeth?

JOHNNY. Lady Macbeth.

TOMMY. No! that's a lady's part. We must play something; what'll it be?

JOHNNY. Let's play tag.

TOMMY. No, no! we must play some piece.

JOHNNY. Let's play on a piece of pie.

TOMMY. No, no! we must play some play as they do in a theatre.

JOHNNY. Oh! I see.

TOMMY. Let me see; there's the Drunkard, a good moral drama.

JOHNNY. You wouldn't have to make up, your nose is so red.

TOMMY. No; that won't do. I have it; we'll play Damon and Pythias. I'll play Damon and you play Lucimicus.

JOHNNY. All right.

TOMMY. What's the first word you say when you comes on the stage?

JOHNNY. Come on, Macduff!

TOMMY. I see you don't know anything about the piece. You see I am Damon, and I've been arrested for knocking over a peanut stand, and put in the calaboose. I have a friend named Pythias, he says that he'll stop in jail while I go into the country and see my wife and child.

JOHNNY. Yes, but you ain't got no wife!

TOMMY. I only play that I've got a wife.

JOHNNY. You'd better not, fur dey'll take you up for bugle-ary.

TOMMY. It's in the piece. I go into the country and take you with me, but if I don't return at a certain hour, Pythias is excuted in my stead; and while I am in the house, bidding my wife and child farewell, you are in the barn-yard, where you kill my hoss!

JOHNNY. But you ain't got any hoss!

TOMMY. It's in the play!

JOHNNY. Oh! I see.

TOMMY. I come from the house and ask you for my horse, and you say, " Forgive me, master, I slew your horse! "

JOHNNY. That's my part, is it?

TOMMY. Yes; get over there!

JOHNNY. (*Repeats h's part a number of times.*) Forgive me, massa, I slew your hoss!

TOMMY. Is that the way to stand? you ought to tremble. (JOHNNY *trembles.*) That's it; keep that shake up. (TOMMY *goes off* L., *and rushes on again.*) 'Tis o'er, Lucimicus: bring thou forth my horse! I've staid too long, and speed must leave the winds behind me. By all the gods, the sun is rushing down the West—

JOHNNY. Let her rush.

TOMMY. Why dost thou stand there? bring thou forth my horse.

JOHNNY. Golly, I've forgot my part!

TOMMY. Slave!

JOHNNY. You call me a slave agin, and I'll bust you in the horn!

TOMMY. Why didn't you say, " Forgive me, master, I slew your horse! "

JOHNNY. I forgot all about it.

TOMMY. Try it once more. Where's that shake? (*Goes off as before.*) Be swift of speech, as my heart is my horse, I say!

JOHNNY. Forgive me, massa, I slew your donkey!

TOMMY. Aha! I'm standing here—

JOHNNY: So am I.

TOMMY. To see if the great gods will with their lightnings execute my prayer upon thee! But be thy punishment mine. I'll tear thee all to pieces! Come!

JOHNNY. Where?

TOMMY. To the eternal river of the dead; the way is
shorter than to Syracuse or Utica. With one swing I'll throw
thee to Tartarus, and follow after thee! Come, Pythias' red
ghost beckons me on. Come, craven! come! come! (*Exit,
dragging* JOHNNY *off* L. H. E.)

JOSH BILLINGS ON THE MULE.

THE mule is half hoss, and half jackass, and then kums
tu a full stop, natur diskovering her mistake. Tha weigh
more, akordin tu their heft, than enny other kreetur, except
a crowbar. Tha kant hear enny quicker, nor further than
the hoss, yct their ears are big enuff for snow shoes. You
ken trust them with enny one whose life ain't worth enny
more than the mule's. The only wa tu keep them into a
paster, is tu turn them into a medder jineing, and let them
jump out. Tha are reddy for use, just as soon as they will
du tu abuse. Tha haint got enny friends, and will live on
huckel-berry brush, with an ockasional chanse at Kanada
thissels. Tha are a modern invenshun, i dont think the Bible
deludes tu them at tall. Tha sel for more mony than enny
other domestik animile. Yu kant tell their age by looking
into their mouth, enny more than you kould a Mexican
cannon's. Tha never hav no disease that a good club wont
heal. If tha ever die tha must kum rite tu life agin, for i
never herd nobody sa "ded mule." Tha are like sum men,
very korrupt at harte; ive known them tu be good mules for
6 months, just tu git a good chanse to kick sombody. I never
owned one, nor never mean to, unless there is a United
Staits law passed, requiring it. The only reason why tha
are pashunt, is bekause tha are ashamed ov themselfs. I
have seen eddikated mules in a sirkus. Tha kould kick, and
bite, tremenjis. I would not sa what I am forced tu sa again
the mule, if his birth want an outrage, and man want tu
blame for it. Enny man who is willing tu drive a mule,

ought to be exempt by law from running for the legislatur. Tha are the strangest creeturs on earth, and heaviest, ackording tu their sise; I herd tell ov one who fell oph from the tow path, on the Eri kanawl, and sunk as soon as he touched bottom, but he kept rite on towing the boat tu the nex stashun, breathing thru his ears, which stuck out ov the water about 2 feet 6 inches; i didn't see this did, but an auctioneer told me ov it, and i never knew an auctioneer tr lie unless it was absolutely convenient.

THE TINKER AND THE GLAZIER.

HARRISON.

SINCE gratitude, 'tis said, is not o'er common,
  And friendly acts are pretty near as few,
With high and low, with man, and eke with woman,
  With Turk, with Pagan, Christian, and with Jew;
We ought, at least, when'er we chance to find
  Of these rare qualities a slender sample,
To show they may possess the human mind,
And try the boasted influence of example.
Who knows how far the novelty may charm?
At all events it cannot do much harm.
The tale we give, then, and we need not fear,
The moral, if there be one, will appear.

Two thirsty souls met on a sultry day,
  One glazier Dick, the other Tom the tinker;
Both with light purses, but with spirits gay,
  And hard it were to name the sturdiest drinker.
      Their ale they quaff'd;
    And as they swigg'd the nappy,
        They both agreed, 'tis said,
        That trade was wondrous dead,
      They joked, sung, laughed,
    And were completely happy.

The landlord's eye, bright as his sparkling ale,
  Glisten'd to see them the brown pitcher hug;

For ev ry jest, and song, and merry tale,
   Had this blithe ending—" Bring us t'other mug ! "
Now Dick the glazier feels his bosom burn,
To do his friend Tom Tinker a good turn ;
And where the heart to friendship feels inclin'd,
Occasion seldom loiters long behind.
The kettle, gayly singing on the fire,
Gives Dick a hint just to his heart's desire ;
And, while to draw more ale the landlord goes,
Dick in the ashes all the water throws ;
   Then puts the kettle on the fire again,
      And at the tinker winks,
      As " Trade success ! " he drinks,
   Nor doubts the wish'd success Tom will obtain.
Our landlord ne'er could such a toast withstand ;
So giving each kind customer a hand,
      His friendship too display'd,
      And drank—" Success to trade ! "
But, oh ! how pleasure vanish'd from his eye,
   How long and rueful his round visage grew,
Soon as he saw the kettle bottom fly,
   Solder the only fluid he could view !
He raved, he caper'd, and he swore,
And damn'd the kettle's body o'er and o'er.
" Come, come," says Dick, " fetch us, my friend, more ale.
   All trade you know must live ;
Let's drink—' May trade with none of us e'er fail !
   The job to Tom then give ;
And, for the ale he drinks, my lad of metal,
Take my word for it, soon will mend your kettle."
The landlord yields ; but hopes 'tis no offence
To curse the trade that thrives at his expense.
Tom undertakes the job ; to work he goes,
And just concludes it with the evening's close.
Souls so congenial had friends Tom and Dick,
   They might be fairly called brother and brother.
Thought Tom, " To serve my friend I know a trick,
   And one good turn always deserves another."
      Out now he slily slips,

But not a word he said,
The plot was in his head,
And off he nimbly trips,
Swift to the neighboring church his way he takes;
Nor in the dark,
Misses his mark,
But ev'ry pane of glass he quickly breaks
But as he goes,
His bosom glows,
To think how great will be his friend Dick's joy
At getting so much excellent employ.
Return'd, he beckoning draws his friend aside,
Importance in his face,
And, to Dick's ear his mouth applied,
Thus briefly states the case :
" Dick, I may give you joy; you're a made man ;
I've done your business most complete, my friend :
I'm off—the devil catch me, if he can—
Each window of the church you've got to mend;
Ingratitude's worst curse on my head fall,
If for your sake I have not broke them all."
Tom, with surprise, sees Dick turn pale;
Who deeply sighs—" Oh, la ! "
Then drops his under jaw,
And all his powers of utterance fail;
While horror in his ghastly face,
And bursting eye-balls, Tom can trace;
Whose sympathetic muscles, just and true,
Share, with his heart,
Dick's unknown smart,
And two such phizzes ne'er met mortal view.
At length friend Dick his speech regain'd,
And soon the mystery explain'd—
" You have indeed my business done !
And I, as well as you, must run ;
For, let me act the best I can,
Tom, Tom, I am a ruined man !
zounds, zounds ! this piece of friendship costs me dear.
I always mend church windows *by the year !* "

WONDERFUL DREAM.

A NEGRO DIALOGUE.

CHRISTY.

JULIUS. Sam, did you eber go huntin' in the winter time way out West?

SAM. No, Julius.

JULIUS. Well, I have, Sam.

SAM. You enjoyed yourself, I suppose?

JULIUS. Oh, yes. Ebery time I went I had lots ob fun, until de last time I went—den I had bad luck.

SAM. How happened that?

JULIUS. Well, you see dar was two ob my neighbors come to me an' axed me fur to go huntin' wid ems, an' I said I would go. So we all got our tings ready to start, and I noticed de oder fellers had an extra game bag all filled wid somefin, and says I, "Fellers, what you got dar?" Dey said "Eatments!" and would you believe it, Sam, I had forgot to get anyting ready fur to take wid me for to eat.

SAM. That was a great oversight on your part.

JULIUS. Yes; but dey stopt to a hotel till I went back to my dwelling and got some provender, and I didn't know how much dey had, so I bought a loaf of bread extra, and hid it under my arm, and buttoned my coat ober it.

SAM. Why, Julius, dey must have discovered it.

JULIUS. Oh, no, Sam; de place where my heart used to be before I got dis'pointed in lub, was big enuff to hide de bread. Well, Sam, we got way out in de wild wilderness, and arter we'd bin dar for free or four weeks, we found out dat our eatments wouldn't last.

SAM. Then you was in a perdicament.

JULIUS. No, we was in de woods.

SAM. Well, what did you do?

JULIUS. I couldn't do nofin; but I had my loaf ob bread and, somehow or oder, dese fellers found out dat I had it aud dey was jealous.

SAM. How did you manage? did you divide it?

JULIUS. What, Sam! divide a tree cent loaf twixt tree ob us?—no sir. Any one ob us felt as if we could eat it vridout chawin'. So I proposed dat we should all go to sleep, and de one dat dream de biggest dream should hab de loaf ob bread.

SAM. What were the dreams?

JULIUS. One dreampt dat he seen a kettle dat was so big dat dey had to git a ladder seventeen thousand feet long fur to git into it.

SAM. That was a large dream.

JULIUS. Yes, but de oder feller beat him.

SAM. What was his dream?

JULIUS. He got up and dreampt—

SAM. No, no; he dreamed—got up and told his dream

JULIUS. Yes; dat's what I said; he dreamed dat he seen a cabbage so big, dat it covered four thousand acres ob ground.

SAM. That did beat the other dream, truly.

JULIUS Yes, it did, Sam.

SAM. What was your dream?

JULIUS. Well, Sam, I dreamed dat in de middle ob de night I got hungry, and eat up de bread, and my dream come true.

A NEW OCCASIONAL ADDRESS.

FOR A LADY'S FIRST APPEARANCE.

SPOKEN BY MRS. JOHNSTONE.

WHEN the bleak winds in winter's hoary reign,
Bind up the waters in his icy chain;
When round the pool village the youngsters meet,
And try the frozen edge with tim'rous feet,
The surface trembles and the crackling noise
Cows with wide-spreading fear faint-hearted boys;
Whilst one more vent'rous than the rest appears,
Glides to the centre, and assur'd it bears,

Rais'd on his skates, the polish'd mirror skims,
Nor dreads immersion deep, bruis'd bones, or broken limbs,
Just such a vent'rer, trembling near tho shore,
Was I, when first I tried this surface o'er.
With doubtful step, new to the slippery stage,
I anxious wished, yet dreaded, to engage.
Hope smiled auspicious, and assurance gave—
I should not meet a cold, o'erwhelming grave;
Then from the shore my puny bark I push'd,
Whilst your applause my loudest terrors hush'd,
And to your candor trusting, still I glide,
Safely my bark 'long the unruffled tide;
Your kind protection is the prosp'rous gale
That speeds its voyage and extends its sail;
And whilst such fav'ring breezes happy blow,
With all the aid indulgence can bestow,
Be *this* her wished-for course—her grateful name,
The Endeavor brig, bound for the port of Fame.

AN OCCASIONAL PROLOGUE.

TO BE SPOKEN AT THE OPENING OF PERFORMANCE.

THE stoic's plan is futile, which requires
Our wants supplied by lopping our desires.
As well by this vague scheme might we propose,
Cut off your feet, 'twill save the price of shoes.
As well might we thus courting public favor,
To gain your plaudits, lop off all endeavor.
The thought we spurn: be it our constant aim
By assiduity to gain a name,
Your approbation points the road to fame;
Each effort use, nor e'er a moment pause,
To reap that golden harvest—your applause.
Sweet is the balm which *hope's* kind aid bestows,
To lighten grief, or mitigate our woes;
To raise desponding merit, banish fear;
And from the trembler wipe the falling tear;

To diffidence inspire, it's dread beguile,
And doubt extinguish with a cheering smile ;
That task be yours.   My co-mates with some dread,
Depute me here, their willing cause to plead ;
Your fiat must our future fates control,
For here, our chief has " garner'd up his soul ;"
Eager to please, his throbbing heart beats high,
By you depress'd, or swelled to ecstacy ;
Then bid the phantom Fear at once depart,
And rapture revel in his anxious heart.

ADDRESS ON CLOSING A PERFORMANCE.

As when on closing of a well-spent life,
The parting *husband* views his faithful wife
(For life itself is but a gaudy play,
The flutt'ring phantom of a summer's day),
With pleasing terror and with trembling haste,
He recollects a thousand raptures past ;
And though resign'd, and conscious that he must
Delay to mingle with his kindred dust ;
So I, while round these seats my sight I bend,
And in each cordial eye behold a friend,
From the fond flowings of a grateful heart,
Cannot refrain to cry—Ah ! must we part ?
Your minds, where conscious worth and goodness live,
May paint the boundless thanks we wish to give,
But it's beyond the power of words to tell,
The *debt* we owe—the *gratitude* we feel.

PROLOGUE.

FOR A PERFORMANCE BY BOYS.

DEAR friends, we thank you for your condescension,
In deigning thus to lend us your attention ;
And hope the various pieces we recite
(Boys though we are) will yield you some delight.

From wisdom and from knowledge, pleasure springs,
Surpassing far the glaring pomp of kings :
All outward splendor quickly dies away,
But wisdom's honors never can decay.

Blest is the man who treads her paths in youth,
They lead to virtue, happiness and truth ;—
Sages and patriots in these ways have trod,
Saints have walked in them till they reached their God.

The powers of eloquence can charm the soul,
Inspire the virtuous, and the bad control ;
Can rouse the passions, or their rage can still,
And mould a stubborn mob to one man's will.

Such powers the great Demosthenes attained,
Who haughty Philip's conquering course restrained
Indignant thundering at his country's shame,
Till every breast in Athens caught the flame.

Such powers were Cicero's :—with patriot might
He dragged the lurking treason forth to light,
Which long had festered in the heart of Rome,
And saved his country from her threatened doom.

Nor to the senate or the bar confined,
The pulpit shows its influence o'er the mind ;
Such glorious deeds can eloquence achieve ;
Such fame, such deathless laurels, it can give.

Then say not this our weak attempt is vain,
For frequent practice will perfection gain,
The fear to speak in public it destroys,
And drives away the bashfulness of boys.

Various the pieces we to-night repeat,
And in them various excellences meet,
Some rouse the soul—some gently soothe the ear
" From grave to gay, from lively to severe."

We would your kind indulgence then bespeak,
For awkward manner, and for utterance weak,
Our powers, indeed, are feeble; but our aim
Is not to rival Greek or Roman fame.

Our sole ambition aims at your applause,
We are but young—let youth, then, plead our cause.
And if your approbation be obtained,
Our wish is answered, and our end is gained.

EPILOGUE.

FOR A SCHOOL PERFORMANCE.

Our parts are perform'd and our speeches are ended,—
    We are monarchs, courtiers, and heroes no more;
To a much humbler station again we've descended,
    And are now but the school-boys you've known us before.

Farewell then our greatness—'tis gone like a dream,
    'Tis gone—but remembrance will often retrace
The indulgent applause which rewarded each theme,
    And the heart-cheering smiles that enliven'd each face.

We thank you!—Our gratitude words cannot tell,
    But deeply we feel it—to you it belongs;
With heartfelt emotion we bid you farewell,
    And our feelings now thank you much more than our tongues.

We will strive to improve, since applauses thus cheer us,
    That our juvenile efforts may gain your kind looks;
And we hope to convince you the next time you hear us,
    That praise has but sharpened our relish for books.

FINALE.

THE pages that in Humor's train
  Have well performed their jolly function,
Should not be parted with, 'tis plain,
  Without a little comic unction.
And so our book, in which they've passed
  The reader's eye, in gay succession,
Shall wind up with a joke, at last,
  In honor of the quaint procession:
Why is this work like regions wild
  Of which our fox hunters are lovers?
Because there is—to draw it mild—
  Most glorious sport within the covers!